CUM ON FEEL THE NOIZE!
THE STORY OF SLADE

ACKNOWLEDGEMENTS

The Authors would like to thank:

Robert Kirby & Catherine Cameron at PFD, Lorna Russell at Carlton Books, Judy Totton, Natalie at Ignition Management, Mark Brennan at Captain Oi!, Stephen at Rex Features, Phil Hendriks (The Young Guitar), Andy Street at Universal Records, Steve Woof at EMI Records, Bill Ellis at A and B Management, and Suzi Quatro.

Alan would like to thank:

Mum, David Parker, Amy Palmer (Elvis's Moody Blue album track two), Jake Burns, Ian McCallum, Ali McMordie, Mick O'Shea, Steve Diggle, Jerry White, Terry Rawlings, Robert Ross, Matt Martin, Gary Carverhill, Jon McCaughey, Jon Richards, Roxanne, Hannah, Liza, Sarah, Nomtai, Steve Gowans, Don Letts, Martin Baker, Sean at Helter Skelter, Paul Roberts, Simon Leppington, Mik Wilkojc, Sid Griffin, Ian Preece and Ian Marshall at Orion Books, Nick Reynolds, Bruce Reynolds, Craig Orrick, Jo and all at The Spice of Life, rock'n'roll Ray Morrissey, Gary Crowley, Welsh Pete, Steve Burch and Bob Ramsey.

Steve would like to thank:

John Magner for text suggestions; Sarah Vauls, without whom this book would not have been possible, for extensive research and proofreading; Craig Adams for insider information; James Stevenson for archive material; Sean Body for invaluable lessons; and Mum and Dad for support.

Sources

NME, Record Mirror, Sounds, Look-In, Jackie, Rolling Stone, Cream, The Slade Story (BBC Television), *Slade Alive!* (DVD), *Glam Rock: 20th Century Rock & Roll* by Dave Thompson, Collector's Guide Publishing; *Noddy Holder: Who's Crazee Now*, Ebury Press

The publishers would like to thank the following sources for their kind permission to reproduce the pictures in this book.

Getty Images: /Evening Standard: 105; /Express Newspapers: 130; /Terry O'Neill/Hulton Archive: 60

Private Collection: 152 bl

Redferns: /Jorgen Angel: 53; /EMI Archives: 18, 22; /Michael Ochs Archives: 23; /Jim Sharpe: 141

Retna Pictures Ltd.: /M. Webster: 99

Rex Features: 6, 10, 12, 13, 14, 17, 21, 69, 71, 80, 87, 112, 115, 116, 138, 148; /Eugene Adebari: 85 br; /Dave Allocca: 78; /Roger Bamber: 5, 58, 66, 81 tr, 82, 83, 84, 92, 94, 95, 101, 111, 137, 150, 152 tr; /Jacques Bernard: 9, 74; /John Bryson: 72, 114; /Chris Capstick: 117, 118, 120, 147; /Andre Csillag: 40, 51, 62, 67, 108, 109, 124, 127, 144, 153, 154; /David Dagley: 97; /Everett Collection: 106; /Globe Photos Inc: 42; /Harry Goodwin: 20 l, 20 c, 20 r, 37, 38, 39, 47, 54, 73, 119, 156; /Dezo Hoffmann: 28, 32, 34, 35, 45, 48, 52, 57, 102, 143; /London Weekend Television: 49, 85 tl, 121; /David Magnus: 27; /Lynne McAfee: 132, 135; /Brian McCreeth: 64, 98; /Brian Moody: 63, 107, 76-77; /Ilpo Musto: 81 bl, 133; /News Group: 123; /Dick Polak: 104; /Mark Putland: 129; /John Selby: 25, 89, 90; /Ray Stevenson: 31; /Ken Williams: 68

Every effort has been made to acknowledge correctly and contact the source and/or copyright holder of each picture and Carlton Books Limited apologises for any unintentional errors or omissions which will be corrected in future editions of this book.

CUM ON FEEL THE *NOIZE!*
THE STORY OF SLADE

Alan Parker & Steve Grantley

CARLTON
BOOKS

This book is dedicated to Henry 'Harry' Parker (1927-2005)

THIS IS A CARLTON BOOK

First published by in Great Britain by Carlton Books Limited 2006
20 Mortimer Street
London W1T 3JW

10-digit ISBN 1 - 84442-151-1
13-digit ISBN 978-1-84442-151-0

Printed in Dubai

CONTENTS

FOREWORD

by Suzi Quatro

They were a dying breed of real musicians gigging every gig God sent, in and out of the Watford Gap, indulging in midnight feasts of grease, caffeine and smoke, doing the milk-run back to Wolverhampton, where bed and breakfast at Mum's was free. After the Sixties had disappeared in acid and marijuana, it was all about the unrelenting drum beat, often double-tracked, the loud guitars (permanently on 11), the shrill vocals and the catchy tunes, not to mention the six-storey platform boots, long hair and make-up, huge bell-bottomed, glittery pants and bomber jackets… And you should have seen the girls!

Slade were about to do their first UK tour and I was champing at the bit to do some gigs, so the legendary hit-maker Mickie Most used his influence to convince Chas Chandler to let us open the show, which also included Thin Lizzy. I would have 20 minutes at the beginning of every show to strut my stuff. Well, I had heard the boys many times on the radio and seen them in various music papers like *The Melody Maker*, *Sounds* and *NME*, and I thought, better get my act together – this ain't gonna be easy. Mickie's wife, Chris, and I rushed down High Street Kensington to get a stage outfit. Now, how could I compete with the boys and all their crazy colours? Well, picture this: pink and green striped glittery bell-bottoms and a beige bomber jacket with huge platform boots and oh yes, pink hair. Yes, *pink* hair. Oh boy, was I gonna be noticed. So, image all in place, we set off up the road to the first gig: Newcastle City Hall.

Now I was told that Slade fans were not very kind to support acts, booing and throwing things, so to say I was a little nervous was an understatement. But Detroit training did me proud and I went up and stormed it. Next came Thin Lizzy, with Phil Lynott strutting up and down like a panther. 'Whiskey In The Jar', great song, but Phil, bless you, you would have been a great guitar player… Anyway, finally the moment came. I stood on the side of the stage and waited while the place began to erupt with impatient fans waiting for their idols.

Boom, boom, boom, boom, boom… Don Powell takes the stage. He was cute, he was dangerous, and he began to pound out that typical Slade beat. When Don hit the drums, they stayed hit. He laid down a locomotive express of rhythm, never letting up for a minute. I do believe he was the most popular with the girls. They just seem to love drummers – maybe it's got something to do with stamina! Enter Dave Hill. Flashy guitarist, all teeth and boots, teetering on boots six inches high (which he managed to fall off during the tour and had to do the remainder in a golden throne, honest), cape flowing and stomping all over the stage in what can only be described as totally entertaining. Oh yes, he was! Jimmy Lea, the most restrained of all, sprayed-on purple satin trousers and semi-stacked boots, he was the real 'muso' of the band, playing excellent melodic bass lines plus violin and piano. Movement wise, he was the anchor, tying everything together. Finally, the star: Mr Charisma was, and is, one of the best. I watched Noddy Holder crawl onto the stage, complete with mirrored top hat, hiding behind the monitors as the crowd went crazy and when he finally stood up, the voice took over. Yes, Noddy has a rock'n'roll voice reminiscent of Little Richard and that is what you call a compliment. Noddy had the audience in the palm of his hands. I was impressed; I learned a lot on that tour.

Of course we all became friends, and still are. Every time Noddy sees me now, he always says two things: 'I watched you and Len Tuckey [my first husband and guitarist] fall in love' and 'Suze, don't ever write a book, cuz you remember *everything*.' Well, I can't promise you that, Noddy, but I will say, 'I love you guys.'

Ladies and gentlemen, please welcome S L A D E.

INTRODUCTION

Slade were undoubtedly the greatest glam rock band ever, but they were also so much more. Never fashionable or hip, they became hugely successful on their own terms and were more influential than many would like to acknowledge. From working class boys playing local clubs and pubs to huge chart success, Slade became a 'Seventies phenomenon. They were one of the most successful pop acts of all time.

Endlessly and effortlessly – or so it seemed – the song-writing team of Holder & Lea produced a string of hits. Their 'good-time-vibe-anthems' and 'scarves-in-the-air' sense of rock balladry lasted them throughout their entire career, their popularity and subsequent longevity relying upon the quality of their songs and the passion in their playing. Slade proved to be so much more than a 'one-trick pony', a criticism levelled at them by many a Seventies rock writer. The band achieved massive success, so much so that they seemed to have a permanent slot on BBC's Top Of The Pops, and releasing the one Christmas single even your granny can remember. They stomped all over the competition, leaving bands like Mud, Sweet, Roy Wood's Wizard and T Rex in their wake. Even the masterful David Bowie and the prolific Elton John couldn't keep up with Slade's runaway success. Slade even featured in their very own movie, 1974's Flame, which was just too gritty and real for its teen-based fan market. Subsequently the film has been recognised as a classic of the genre, with film director and critic Mark Kermode calling Flame 'the greatest British rock movie ever'.

Today, Slade have some unexpected fans, from comedian and writer Ben Elton to Goth rockers The Mission. US heavy metal band Quiet Riot and Brit-Pop kings Oasis have covered their songs, leading bass player Jimmy Lea to comment, 'It's cool that people get it.' In 1975, an effort to break into new territory, Slade relocated to the USA for two years. This failed; when they returned home to the UK in 1977, punk rock had all but taken over the music business. It seemed as if their time had passed, yet Slade kept on playing and releasing records. They never lost their power and skill in the live arena, and continued to thrill audiences wherever they performed.

Few bands can boast two successful careers, but after a triumphant return at the Reading Festival in August 1980, Slade did just that. They experienced a huge resurgence in their popularity and created even more hits. With each passing year their legacy remains and matures, and reveals them as true pop legends. It could be argued that somewhere between Elvis, Little Richard, The Beatles and ABBA, Slade lurk in the shadows as worthy pop rivals. At their peak they sold 50 million records worldwide, including six No. 1 singles in the Seventies – a record equalled only by Swedish phenomenon ABBA. They recorded 20 studio albums, made an influential film and forged an unrivalled live reputation, and most of all they became much-loved Seventies heroes. But Slade didn't only become household names – they became part of the very fabric of British life itself. As a nation, it seems that 35 years after their first hit single 'Get Down And Get With It' was released, we are all still Slade crazee!

BLACK COUNTRY BOYS

'We always kept our roots, y'know? You could say you can take the boy out of the Black Country, but you'll never take the Black Country out of the boy.'

Noddy Holder

Donald (Don) George Powell was born on 10 September 1946 in Bilston in the West Midlands. He began his musical career not by playing the drums but the bugle in the Boy Scouts. 'I couldn't play a bugle to save my life,' he commented, many years later. 'I used to stand at the back and fake it, and pray they'd let me be the drummer next week.'

At the age of 13 he began playing drums. He never took any lessons, simply learning by ear. Although a promising athlete, Don knew in his heart that what he really wanted to do was to play drums in a rock'n'roll band. He banged on the dinner table with his knife and fork, driving everyone crazy with his constant tapping. The young Don was full of ideas, boundless energy and enthusiasm.

Left: Four working class boys from the Black Country.

Don had talent and was spotted at the age of 14 by two local guitar players, John (Johnny) Howells and Mick Marsons. They had cut their musical teeth by learning the instrumental track 'Peanut Vendor', thus arriving at the name The Vendors. In late 1963, Howells and Marsons asked the young drummer to join their group, and Don accepted without a moment's hesitation. He had already decided that he wanted a rock'n'roll life so he never had any doubts. Recognising his son's ambition, Don's father bought him a 'Premier' Drum Kit. Until then he had been using a kit borrowed from a friend.

With Don Powell in the group Howells and Marsons became more committed to giving The Vendors their best shot. The band did some local gigs in clubs and pubs, and began to gain some experience. Although the line-up of The Vendors sporadically changed, it remained based around the reputation as a bit of a whiz kid. Dave was asked to join The Vendors and he accepted.

By early 1964 the band decided that now was the time to actually try and record something. In later years, articles on Slade would claim The Vendors' first demo was recorded in singer John Howells' front room. This is incorrect; recording time was booked at the Domino Studios just outside Wolverhampton and The Vendors demoed four songs, the best track being 'Don't leave Me Now', which was composed by singer John Howells and new boy Dave Hill who had joined that year.

The demo worked well for the band and before long they had secured a manager, Maurice Jones, and a booking agent, The Astra Agency run by Stan Fielding and Len Rowe. Once more the line-up changed when bass player Dave 'Cass' Jones was drafted in. He was one of the finest bass players in the area, giving the band had its strongest line-up to date. At this point they became interested in American Blues and their heroes were John Lee Hooker, Howlin' Wolf and Matt 'Guitar' Murphy. With this new-found music came longer hair, Cuban heeled boots and velvet jackets. A name change followed, with The Vendors becoming The 'N Betweens.

The group worked as a semi-pro outfit on the local circuit. They would go to The St Giles Youth Club for what was known then as a 'Shindig' or 'Hop', where the pop groups of the day would play. They quickly became friends with John Squires, the man who ran the place, and he arranged for them to support all of the acts that he booked to play at the youth club. By the middle of 1964 the 'N Betweens had supported such famous names as The Hollies, The Merseybeats, Alexis Korner, Georgie Fame, Spencer Davies and The Yardbirds. Eventually more and more bookings were acquired, and when they secured a Monday night residency at The Plaza in Birmingham in the spring of 1964, the band made the big decision to give up their day jobs.

A&R man Bobby Graham, former drummer with Joe Brown And The Bruvvers and a former booking agent, auditioned The Vendors at Birmingham's Le Metro Club in for French-based Barclay Records. He liked what he saw, and teamed up with Maurice Jones to co-manage The 'N Betweens in mid-1965.

David John Hill. Guitar.

Donald George Powell. Drums.

core of Johnny, Don and Mick. When the band were once more looking for a guitar player, the name Dave Hill came up.

David John Hill was born on 4 April 1946 at Fleet Castle in Devon. As a small boy his family relocated to the Midlands and the young Dave, influenced by many of the skiffle groups, began to play guitar. He became very good very quickly, playing guitar in a local band called The Young Ones, where he earned himself a

Barclay Records organised a recording session at PYE Studios to lay down enough tracks for an EP. Back in those days, there was no such thing as a single in France, just the EP and the LP. The PYE session was recorded in London in the autumn of 1964 andthe finished tracks shipped to Barclay Records; a four-song EP was issued the following winter, but nothing much came of it, and the band languished in obscurity. Oddly enough, no records were ever sent to the group members, and it was not until the late Seventies that John Howells was finally given a copy by a hardcore Slade fan.

In October 1964, The 'N Betweens returned briefly to Wolverhampton before The Astra Agency shipped them off to Germany for a month, until extra work could be found in the UK. The group sailed to Ostend, Holland, before driving to Dortmund via Belgium. Mid-trip they became lost and decided to stop at a snack bar. Just then another van pulled in and a head popped out, shouting, 'Oi! You lot! Wot you doing 'ere?' The van in question belonged to fellow Midlands band Steve Brett & The Mavericks, and the voice was one Noddy Holder.

Neville (Noddy) John Holder was born in Walsall in the West Midlands on the 15 June 1946. The rowdy frontman's career had early beginnings: Noddy's debut as a singer was at the Walsall Labour Club when he was only seven years old. This wasn't a one-off; from then on, he would get up on stage regularly and belt out songs from the hit parade. He loved being up there on stage, the centre of attention. A self-confessed show-off, Noddy had all the prerequisites of a lead singer, except perhaps for the good looks. However, he more than made up for this in charisma and even at this tender age, he oozed confidence.

Noddy's love for music came from his dad, who bought all the hit records of the day. His father was always singing around the house and would often get up at the local workingmen's club and give them a song. Although pretty good, he never took himself seriously as a singer. His son, however, was to develop his own talent.

Noddy had got his nickname from a young school friend who had started calling him 'Noddy' because he would always nod his head in class rather than say

Neville John Holder. Vocals and Guitar.

'yes'. The name stuck. Until that point the cheeky young rascal had been known as 'Neville the Devil'.

When he was nine Noddy went on his own to see the rock'n'roll movie *Rock Around The Clock* (1956). It blew his mind. His very first rock gig was The Everly Brothers with Little Richard in support, and amazingly The Rolling Stones as openers. He once referred to Little Richard as the 'coolest man alive' and, after he saw Elvis Presley in *Jailhouse Rock* (1956) and *King Creole* (1958) it was rock'n'roll from then on. At the age of 12 his parents gave him a second-hand acoustic guitar as a Christmas present and with that he knew what he wanted to be. A rocker was born.

Noddy's very first band, The Phantoms, was formed when he was still in his early teenage years, and, like most first bands, consisted simply of school friends. But unlike many teenage outfits they soon progressed to pubs and clubs, where they were taken seriously and built up a strong reputation. Already he was earning money from being a musician. He was good, and he knew it. As he said in his autobiography, *Who's Crazee Now?*, he had 'found his niche'.

A small-time local celebrity, singer Steve Brett had had his own local TV show *For Teenagers Only*, on which The Beatles had performed. In 1964, he asked The Phantoms, who had recently become The Memphis Cut Outs, to join forces with him and his back-up band, The Mavericks. They released a series of singles on Columbia records without a hit. They did, however, record with legendary producer Joe Meek, responsible for The Tornado's world-wide instrumental hit 'Telstar' (1962) and the pop ditty 'Have I The Right' for The Honeycombs (1964), but none of these recordings were ever released.

Don Powell and Dave Hill were more than aware of Steve Brett and The Mavericks. With Brett a bit of a local celebrity, their reputation preceded them – and in any case, all the local bands knew of each other because they would often end up on the same bill.

Don and Dave had begun to grow tired of the 'N Betweens' direction, and they felt they needed a change of line-up. So when they all got chatting on the ferry to Germany, Don and Dave asked Noddy to join the 'N Betweens. But, happy with Steve Brett, Noddy had refused.

Finally, in early 1964, the 'N Betweens arrived at Habenera Club in Dortmund where the hours were long and sometimes found them playing seven hours a day. Living conditions were atrocious as they were staying in nothing more than an old farmhouse. Don Powell recalled that they 'lived on chicken and chips.' When their time was up they quickly travelled back to the UK. On their return 'Cass' Jones quit the group and an advertisement was placed in the *Wolverhampton Express & Star* for a bass guitar player. Compared to Dave Hill and Don Powell, the young James Whild Lea was a rank amateur, but the band immediately saw he was hugely talented.

James (Jim) Whild Lea was born on the 14 June 1949 in the West Midlands town of Wolverhampton. He was a precocious talent from a musical family. Classically trained, he played the violin, cello, bass and piano. Jim studied hard and earned a place in the Stafford Youth Orchestra but really, music came easy to him. He was a technically proficient musician with a great talent for learning things by ear, working out parts from records with ease.

His favourite local band was the 'N Betweens, who played straight-ahead blues and had built a solid reputation as a good live act. So although he was still in schoo, when he saw the advertisement in the local paper he knew he just had to apply. His audition was held at The Blue Flame Club in Wolverhampton. Now called Lafayette, many years later Slade would return to hold court there as local rock royalty.

Jim turned up for his audition in early 1966 with his bass guitar in a plastic bag, he was way ahead of all those who auditioned that day. The job was instantly his and he was thrilled. Jim joined the band but soon realised that all was not well: there was tension between singer Johnny Howells and the other lads in the group. In Jim's opinion the 'N Betweens were the best band in the area, and he loved Howells' voice, which he thought had an authentic blues quality. He was a good harmonica player too, and Jim couldn't understand why there was a problem.

But the fact was that Don and Dave had grown tired of the narrow range of the music they played. The blues material they had loved when they first discovered it was starting to feel like a straitjacket. But the blues was all Johnny wanted to play, and so inevitably the frustration grew.

Meanwhile, by Christmas 1965, Noddy had returned from Germany and had quit Steve Brett And The Mavericks. He'd had a wild old time in Germany but was starting to get frustrated with being Brett's sidekick. They would share the lead vocal duties but there was a feeling stirring deep inside the singer. He didn't want to be second to anyone. There had also been arguments over money. Without a care, Noddy decided to leave Brett's employ. He was still in his teens.

Noddy bumped into Don and Dave on Wolverhampton High Street in early 1966 and this time accepted their offer to join their band, although somewhat reluctantly. He wanted to be the front man and lead singer – he had had more than enough of backing up Steve Brett and now it turned out that the 'N Betweens already had their own lead singer. Noddy realized he would have to play second fiddle, singing back-up and second guitar, which was not an ideal situation. But he went along with it because he knew Don and Dave wanted to develop their own music beyond copying other groups, and beyond the constraints of their blues roots. Although Don and Dave were excited by the possibilities of this potential new line-up, the young bass player Jimmy Lea hadn't heard of Noddy Holder, and he reserved judgement for now.

The new band had their first ever rehearsal in late February 1966 just across the road from Noddy's house, in the Three Men In A Boat pub just outside Wolverhampton. The chemistry worked immediately. Soon afterwards, their first shopping trip together found them choosing outfits no other band would wear. They bought outrageously garish clothes with bright colours, Dave Hill leading the way with Noddy coming a close second. Don and Jimmy joined in somewhat less enthusiastically, however, and Johnny refused the outlandish stage look altogether and continued to wear his dark suits. The die was cast on that first trip and although their glam years were a way off yet, it was the shape of things to come.

The 'N Betweens started out their professional life in earnest, playing tough local pubs and clubs, where early on they learned valuable lessons that would stand them in good stead for the journey to stardom that lay ahead. The Midlands was an industrial area, hard and uncompromising, but many world-beating bands were born of this brutal landscape. Led Zeppelin's Robert Plant and the mighty John Bonham hailed from these parts, as did drumming legend Cozy Powell and prototype heavy metal band Black Sabbath. Don Powell would go and watch John Bonham in his pre-Zeppelin days when Bonham was playing in a local cabaret band. He was always impressed by his power and would try to emulate that approach himself. Bonham remains his favourite drummer of all time.

It wasn't long before it became clear that the band all wanted to sack Johnny Howells, but for the time being their hands were tied. They had gigs booked six months ahead, and Johnny was what the promoters expected. After that, it would still be many years of struggle and hard work before Slade would emerge as the band we know and love today.

James Whild Lea. Bass, Violin and Piano.

THE 'N BETWEENS

'It was five years before we got any kind of record success. We slogged around the country in the back of a van, sharing bags of chips and things like that.'

Don Powell

The 'N Betweens played their first show as the 'N Betweens on 1 April 1966 at the Walsall Town Hall. Noddy Holder recalled, 'April Fools Day, and we've been playing the fool from then on.' Things came together rapidly, and they quickly picked up residencies at local hotels and pubs. On Sundays the group would play at the Aldridge Community Centre and do what they described as their 'Sunday Service'. This featured Noddy dressed up as a vicar telling dirty jokes in between songs. A natural-born entertainer who basked in the limelight, the singer had no fear of an audience. He had the ability to break down the barrier between audience and band by getting the crowd involved, and he really knew how to engage people.

Left: The 'N Betweens. Young lads with big rock 'n' roll dreams.

The group's first big gig was at Wolverhampton Civic Hall in the spring of 1966, where they supported Cream. They went on to support local band The Move, featuring Roy Wood, who would go on to have success with his own glam band Wizard. The band knew the boys in The Move because they all came from the same area. Noddy also knew Bonham and Robert Plant, who would go on to form Led Zeppelin, and he even roadied once or twice for Plant when he was in a group called Listen. They also supported the earthier John Mayall's Blues Breakers and worked with The Idle Race featuring a young Jeff Lynne, who would go on to form the hit-making machine The Electric Light Orchestra with musical partner Roy Wood.

The lads began to play further afield, taking bookings in Plymouth, Newquay (Roger Taylor from Queen was the drummer in the 'N Betweens opening act on one of their early dates there) and Torquay.

Chapter 2

The changing faces of Roy Wood. Sixties. Hippy. Glam.

After a week in Torquay the band were booked to play four gigs in Newquay and then one in Plymouth. Knowing he was going to be sacked, Johnny Howells quit the group just before they set off for Plymouth. Johnny only wanted to sing Rhythm & Blues. He wasn't interested in pop music, he didn't wear the same clothes as the rest of the boys and he stopped turning up for rehearsals. There was a breakdown in the relationship between him and the other members of the band. For their part, the band was delighted with his departure and relished gigging without him – it was like being set free.

The Plymouth show was their first as a four-piece, and it went down a storm. For a while the band searched for a second singer, believing they needed one, and Robert Plant's name was even mentioned. Don and Dave were finally convinced Noddy could front the band after their roadie Graham Swinerton ('Swin') said he thought Noddy was more than

capable of carrying the show all on his own.

The 'N Betweens gigged regularly as a four-piece and the shows became better and better. Any thoughts of a second singer disappeared forever. The Astra Agency still represented them; being the only real rock'n'roll outfit, they were different to many of the other bands on their roster, and they were glad to have them. The band worked directly with Maurice Jones, who would eventually became their manager, and went on to start his own promotions company, the legendary MCP.

From a technical point of view the band's sound began to develop when they experimented with the important idea of rc-wiring amps to create their own PA (personal address) system. In those days bands would have a small PA system just for vocals, and the guitars and keyboards had their own amplifiers and speaker cabinets behind them on stage. This meant that if you were on one side of the stage all you could hear would be bass guitar and vocals, but

Local band, The Move.

if you happened to be on the other side you would hear nothing but guitars and keyboards. The drums would often be left 'acoustic', or perhaps one vocal mike would be placed above the drummer, so he too would go through the PA, often drowning out the vocalists. It was hardly the ideal situation.

The 'N Betweens were already known for their powerful sound and, with the help of friend and roadie Swin, they took the whole thing to the next level. Swin and Noddy came up with the idea to link up all the amps on stage so that no matter where you stood you would hear everything equally. This created a wall of sound and brought a power to the band that was revolutionary at a time when big PA systems were still in their infancy. Now Noddy and the boys were a step ahead of the game. Later he would comment that the monster sound they produced on stage amazed even the big groups of the day that they supported, such as The Tremoloes and The Hollies.

At the suggestion of Dave Hill all the guitars would all play 'lead' lines. This meant playing the same line in different octaves, rather than having the bass play the root note, the rhythm guitar play the chord and the lead guitar play the top line; instead they *all* played the top line. This musical trick made the riffs sound strident and so much bigger. These days Heavy Metal bands use this technique all the time, but back then it was revolutionary and became the core of the 'N Betweens' sound. Not only this, but the two guitars played syncopated rhythm parts that together created one pumping groove. With all three guitars playing the lead line and blasting through amps on both sides of the stage, the sound was absolutely massive.

Then there was Noddy's voice, so powerful that it seemed almost inhuman. Often it sounded as if some kind of effect had been used on his voice to enhance it and make it so phenomenal. But that was just his natural sound, one of the best rock'n'roll voices ever.

As Status Quo's Rick Parfitt once said, 'Nobody ever sounded like Noddy!' According to Noddy the other band members' parents warned them, 'You'll never get anywhere with that singer… all he ever does is shout!'

Kim Fowley

The band now had a settled line-up and gigged regularly. They found themselves supporting various acts at Tiles, a small basement club in London's Oxford Street, where it just so happened that one night in mid-1966 an American music producer, Kim Fowley, was in the audience.

An incredibly tall, outrageously wacky West Coast character, Fowley's credentials went way back, having hustled in the music business since 1957. He had produced many hit records, including a big Sixties hit called 'Nut Rocker' for B Bumble and

the Stingers and 'Alley Oop' for The Hollywood Argyles. Fowley had worked with Sandy Nelson of 'Teen Beat' and 'Let There Be Drums' fame, and had even recorded with Frank Zappa on The Mothers of Invention's debut album *Freak Out*. He had created, produced and managed all-girl Rock band The Runaways, whose band members Joan Jett and Lita Ford went on to find success as solo artists. Stadium rockers Kiss recorded two of his songs, 'Do You Love Me?' and 'King Of The Night-Time World', and Alice Cooper was to record a co-write of Fowleys on his 'Welcome To My Nightmare' album *Escape*. Fowley went on to help discover Eighties glam rockers Poison and LA band Guns'n'Roses.

'I'm going to make you guys stars,' was the first thing he said to the band. They were blown away when he announced who he was; this man was a star in his own right and he was interested in them. In his autobiography Noddy said, 'He saw something in us, even in those early days, and that gave us a lot of confidence. He was always telling us, "You guys project". He said it every time he saw us.'

The boys had never met anyone like Fowley before. Although an eccentric hippie, he had a good reputation in the music business. If Fowley asked a record company to listen to a group, they listened. His opinion was respected, and he had the charisma to make people take notice. Meeting him was the best thing that had happened to the 'N Betweens so far.

The band went into the Regent Sound studios in London's Tin Pan Alley with Fowley, where they quickly recorded four songs from their live set. These included American No. 1 hit 'You Better Run', originally written and recorded by The Young Rascals, who also had huge hits with 'Groovin' and 'People Got To Be Free'. On the spur of the moment Fowley and Noddy came up with a song they called 'Evil Witchman' and that was recorded, too. Backed by 'Evil Witchman', 'You Better Run' was released as a single in August 1966 under the name the 'N Betweens on the major record label EMI, a deal negotiated by Fowley. Although it didn't chart nationally, it was a local Midlands hit. Dave Hill admits, 'We tried to get a

Legendary producer and musical svengali Kim Fowley.

local store to stock 500 copies thinking that if we sold them we'd be in the charts. It didn't work, of course. But it was Number 1 in Wolverhampton for six weeks; it kept "Green Green Grass Of Home" by Tom Jones off the top spot.' Their local reputation grew and grew.

Fowley returned to the States in the winter of 1966 to pursue other projects. There was no problem between the two parties; their relationship just came to an end. However, although the professional ties were severed, Fowley would always drop in on Slade's live shows in L.A.. He and the band remained friends, but their professional connection began and ended with the 1966 sessions.

Early in 1967, EMI booked the band into Abbey Road studios to see if they could come up with anything else. Pink Floyd were also there, recording their debut album *Piper at the Gates of Dawn*, but it was The Beatles, who were recording *Sergeant Pepper* in the next studio along, who would prove the greatest inspiration to the band. They were the biggest group in the world, and here were the 'N Betweens recording in the same building!

But although their confidence was boosted yet again simply by being so close to the greatness that was The Beatles, no songs were to emerge from the Abbey Road sessions.

Back To Germany

As The Beatles had done before them, The 'N Betweens found themselves doing the regular British band stint over in Hamburg, Germany, in the spring of 1967. This was a great training arena for young bands who could learn their craft and pay their dues all at the same time. But the hours were long and the audiences sometimes rough. Prostitutes would even ply their trade while the groups played. John Lennon once said, 'It made my vision of hell look good!' Though there was little money to be made, there was a ton of fun to be had and the experience was invaluable.

The band had a month's residency booked in a huge converted cinema called The Star Palace

in Kiel. This was a coastal town and they soon realised what a tough area it was when they noticed that even the waiters carried guns. The 'N Betweens took over from Paul Raven and the Boston Showband. Raven's real name was Paul Gadd and he would go on to become disgraced glam rock singer Gary Glitter. He was going through the same apprenticeship and musical development as the 'N Betweens, a process that had helped build, among many others, The Beatles' expertise. Night after night in German clubs, these bands developed a musical strength that simply could not be found in a rehearsal room.

In the Sixties and Seventies groups and artists learned their trade on the stage. Unlike many bands today, they didn't go to stage or drama school and then audition for a manufactured group. They worked hard and got out into the real world to perform and entertain, and they ended up really knowing what they were doing. Their talent and skill were tried and tested. The 'N Betweens played so many shows that performing would become second nature. By the time they finally made it they were still young, but they had become seasoned professionals.

Many years later Noddy commented, 'You have to remember that in those days you didn't have overnight success through making videos. You had to pay your dues as musicians. Today you have to have a hit video on MTV to sell the record. You can manufacture a band, give them the right look, get the right producer and the right song, record the album, then you make a great video and you take off. Overnight the record can be in the charts, just through marketing alone. The pretty boys and the pretty girls are the ones that take preference – it's just another marketing scam. But I'm used to the old rock'n'roll approach where you had to work your way up. We paid our dues on the road; we had a big live following before we had record success.'

The band would play eight hours a day, from early evening to the small hours of the morning, seven days a week. At weekends they played even longer. It was exhausting, and there was always fighting in the club. The manager of the club didn't like the band. Even though they were popular with the crowd, he said they played too loudly. He wasn't paying them properly, and constantly complained about them. So after three hard weeks they decided to leave and return to Britain. Noddy felt the band had been ripped off, so just before they left he sabotaged the amplifiers that were the club owners' pride and joy. The owner went berserk and swore revenge, but the damage had been done and the band was long gone.

More strongly than the others, Noddy felt he had to get his own back, and he was prepared to take action. This was just another part of the leadership qualities that made him such a fearless frontman.

Back in the UK the 'N Betweens continued to work regularly and built a ferocious live reputation up and down the country. North of the Border their popularity was growing quickly, where they supported The Dream Police, a group that would eventually become Scottish funksters The Average White Band and, eventually, The Sensational Alex Harvey Band. The boys were learning all the time – and the Scottish gigs paid

The Sensational Alex Harvey Band. Slade would support the Scottish rockers in the early days.

well. They began to headline their own shows and on Saturday nights would play two gigs, one in a theatre and later another smaller show at a club. 'They were fantastic days,' says Noddy. Even though there was no fame or fortune, just lots of travelling in their old van and uncomfortable nights in rough guesthouses, they were the real formative years, and possibly among the band's happiest times.

Their reputation continued to spread and The 'N Betweens began to transcend many local peers. They were unlike many of their contemporaries who played pop hits and were little more than cabaret acts. Together Powell, Lea, Hill and Holder were a rowdy rock'n'roll band, and they rocked every single audience they played for. They had something special.

In the summer of 1968, the bands promoter in the Bahamas booked them into a plush hotel and told them to order whatever they wanted on room service and he would pick up the tab. All the hospitality and board at the hotel was compliments of the promoter and his club.

The band were booked into the promoter's club on the other side of Grand Bahama Island. The group's audience changed at midnight from the easy-to-please American and British tourists to the not-so-easliy-saatisfied Bahamians. The band won them over by playing James Brown covers. James Brown was a god on the island and the locals accepted the band because they were playing not only Mr Brown tunes but also Soul and Tamala Motown tracks. The band had no idea that these songs would save them; they simply played their set.

Midway through their two-month engagement, the owner of the club did a runner, leaving the boys with a massive accommodation and bar bill. They owed the hotel a fortune.

When the club was re-opened, the new owner hired the band. The group moved into a staff apartment in the hotel and half of the band's wages each week was given to the hotel to pay off their debts. It took them three whole months to clear the hotel drink and board bill.

Andy Scott, the guitar player who would end up in rival glam rock band Sweet, was in the Bahamas at the same time, playing with a group called The Elastic Band. Unlike the 'N Betweens, his band were playing the good clubs on the island and actually getting paid. There was indeed trouble in paradise for Noddy and the boys, but it wasn't all bad. They made friends with many of the American kids, and these youngsters would lend the band all their new records. This put them ahead of the bands back home who were at least a month or two behind on the latest US releases. Musically, they were stronger than ever from playing every night of the week for four months. They developed new musical skills and took on board more exotic influences such as Calypso.

The 'N Betweens returned to Britain more determined than ever. In the autumn of 1968, they were approached by a new agent, Roger Allen, who secured an audition for them with Fontana records.

London-based Fontana and Polydor were both part of the Philips empire, a company that made electrical goods. Allen introduced them to managing director Jack Baverstock. At their first meeting in Baverstock's luxurious office, he practised his golf putting. Quite calmly and almost without looking up,

he announced that he wanted the band to go into the studio for a week or two to lay down some tracks. There was no need for band or manager to plead or cajole; they didn't even have to sell themselves. He wanted the band: it was that simple.

Although Allen had told the boys that Baverstock was a big fan of the 'N Betweens, this was a lie. The record company executive had never heard of them, so how or why he was so keen to record them no one knows. But the deal was done and, in the winter of 1968, the band found themselves in Fontana's basement studio with professional recording engineers.

The recordings consisted of favourite songs from the band's set and a couple of new tunes that they wrote together. They also covered songs from a variety of artists – there was a Frank Zappa number, plus a Moody Blues track and a song written by Jeff Lyne. All sorts of musical styles were welded together with no continuity of style. This was pretty much their live set. Although this was their big chance and they wanted to make the most of it, they still didn't take themselves too seriously.

The band worked hard for a week from nine in the morning until sometimes six or seven at night, but they had fun all the while. Once a day Baverstock would come down and listen to their progress, but he never said very much. There was a lot riding on this for everyone, and the band was nervous about his reaction to the finished product. When the recordings were finished, Baverstock announced that he wanted to release them as an album. The 'N Betweens thought they were doing demos but no, this was to be an album. So they had a record deal, but it was on one condition: they must change their name. Around this time the band had come up with an alternative name for themselves – Knicky, Knacky, Noo. This idea was, of course, rejected. What were they thinking?

Ambrose Slade

The name Ambrose Slade came from Baverstock's secretary, who insisted on giving inanimate objects silly names. It just so happened that one thing on her desk was called 'Slade' and another 'Ambrose' and the two somehow ended up being put together. Much to the lads' disappointment the band was rechristened 'Ambrose Slade' – they hated it! But they wanted a record deal and were prepared to do anything to get it, so begrudgingly they agreed.

Chas Chandler. Bass player with The Animals, manager of Jimi Hendrix and the mastermind behind Slade's phenomenal success.

The newly-rechristened Ambrose Slade immediately got themselves a London-based agent. They didn't want to lose Roger Allen as he had done so much for them in such a small space of time, but nonetheless he was paid off, and John Gunnell took them on. Gunnell, who first met the band in the winter of 1968, was an agent who looked after various big artists of the day, including Geno Washington and Georgie Fame. He and his brother Rick also owned various night clubs and definitely had clout in the music business – which, at this point, was just what Ambrose Slade needed.

Chas Chandler

As well as being the bass player from The Animals, Chas Chandler is famous for having discovered, managed and produced the legendary guitar player Jimi Hendrix. Having spotted Hendrix at a club in New York's Greenwich Village, he was responsible for bringing him over to the UK from the States, helping turn the unknown Jimi into a legend. Tough as nails and over 6ft tall, Chandler hailed from Newcastle, and was notorious in the music business. A formidable character, his was an old-school approach to management. Recently Gunnell and Chandler had teamed up, and were part of the powerful Robert Stigwood Organisation, a management company who looked after artists such as guitar legend Eric Clapton, among many others. Now, he was looking for another act to manage, so when John Gunnell arranged to meet Ambrose Slade at the Fontana offices he decided to tag along. This was the big break the boys had all been waiting for. With these men on board anything was possible.

Chandler first saw the band play in the winter of 1968 at Rasputin's, a disco club in London. By the time he arrived the crowd were going wild. He knew immediately that they had what it takes to go all the way to the top. In 1973 he told John Ingham of *Rolling Stone* magazine: 'I was supposed to look for new acts and do some record production. One day I had a call from a guy who told me about this group called Slade and that they wanted a manager. I went down to see them and they knocked me out. I was as impressed when I first saw Slade as I was when I first saw Jimi Hendrix.'

After the show Chandler walked into the band's dressing room and signed them up to a management deal on the spot. It was the stuff of dreams. For this bunch of Black Country misfits, Chandler was to be the ultimate salesman. With him at the helm, anything could happen – and usually did. Already a music business veteran, he knew how to get the best for his band. Chandler was to mastermind the band's rise to fame. He employed a press agent

Left: Slade become Bovver Boys. The attention-grabbing new image.

– Keith Altham, who also worked for The Who, Marc Bolan and The Rolling Stones. Together the two men began to think about how they could get their new band some attention.

Beginnings

The first Ambrose Slade album was made up of what they had originally regarded as demos, so it was all recorded and ready to go. Produced by the band with Roger Wake, the in-house engineer at Fontana Studios, it was released in April 1969 and appropriately titled *Beginnings*. Out of the 12 tracks only four are self-penned and two of those are instrumentals. The album opens with an instrumental called 'Genesis', basically a backing track for what would become 'Know Who You Are', which would open their next album, *Play It Loud* (released 1970). Chas Chandler suggested that the track could use a lyric, and Don Powell claims the song is all about Dave Hill.

With its echoes of The Small Faces and The Beatles, *Beginnings* careers from style to style. The band flirt with boogie-woogie and crash-land on 12-bar blues. In parts Noddy sounds like Steve Marriot. At that time he hadn't yet built up enough confidence in his full-on, shouting style and here he actually sings. It's not until you reach the Marvin Gaye cover, 'If This World Were Mine', that he sounds like himself. Jim Lea provides some beautiful violin on the poignant Holder and Lea composition 'Pity The Mother'. Covers include the Frank Zappa tune, 'Ain't Got No Heart', Lennon and McCartney's 'Martha My Dear', and a song from fellow Black Country boy Jeff Lynne entitled 'Knocking Nails Into My House'. There's a contribution from Moody Blues singer Justin Heyward, 'Fly Me High', and the classic Steppenwolf track 'Born To Be Wild'. The album finishes with the Nugent and Farmer song, 'Journey To The Centre Of Your Mind'.

A photoshoot was arranged for *Beginnings* at Pouk Hill in early 1969, a local beauty spot close to Noddy's home in Wolverhampton. Although it was thick with snow, the photographer insisted on shooting the band naked from the waist up – something that would see the whole band laid up with 'flu the following week. 'You couldn't even see the bloody snow when the cover was printed!' Don would complain, many years later. But it wasn't an entirely wasted experience; 'Pouk Hill' would reappear as the title of a song on their next album *Play It Loud*.

A single was released in the May of 1969 featuring the track 'Genesis' backed by Roach Daddy, but it disappeared without trace. Unfortunately, *Beginnings* bombed. Reviewer Lester Bangs of *Phonograph Record* said their first album 'was a real dud.' Considering there was no real direction to the overall concept, with diverse and opposing styles of music, this was not much of a surprise. But although it may have been an inauspicious start, it didn't dent the band's confidence, nor Chandler's faith in them. Singles were regarded as the big prize, and the band remained absolutely convinced they could have a hit record.

Ambrose Slade continued to play live and debuted in some prestigious London venues including The Speakeasy, The Temple, The Red Car Jazz Club and the world-famous Marquee. By now they had supported the still-struggling Elton John, Stone The Crows (featuring Maggie Bell on lead vocals and Leslie Harvey, brother of Alex of The Sensational Alex Harvey Band, on guitar) and Atomic Rooster, whose drummer, Carl Palmer, would go on to become part of the massively successful progressive rock group Emerson, Lake and Palmer. It was all coming together.

However, Chandler and PR man Keith Altham felt that the band didn't have the right image. They needed a change, something that would make them stand out from the crowd. Altham asked, 'What's news? What's causing controversy?' At the time long hair and flares were *de rigueur* in the rock'n'roll world. Jokingly, Altham suggested that they should shave off all their hair and become skinheads. But Chandler took his idea seriously and thought it was the perfect solution.

This presented a huge problem, as none of the lads were enthusiastic about becoming a skinhead band. Don recalled, 'Chas was on the phone saying, "I want you to become skinheads," and I was like, no, no, no! I've spent three years growing this – no way!' Skinheads were linked to football violence and

the group, especially flamboyant Dave Hill, who loved his long hair, wanted to have no part in it. The group had always worn outrageous clothes with crazy hair and they were unwilling to roll over and comply that easily. But Chandler was convinced this was the right direction for the band. He could be very persuasive when he needed to be and he wasn't going to back down. Having gone through a lot himself as an artist, as well as handling the precocious talent and fragile ego of Jimi Hendrix, he had learnt a lot about getting his own way. Hendrix hadn't wanted to record the song 'Hey Joe', but somehow Chandler managed to convince him otherwise. On this occasion he called the lads into his office, and after much persuasion they acquiesced, but they weren't happy. They didn't like their new name, and now they hated the group's new look, too.

The same man who had created Jimi Hendrix's mad Afro hairstyle was the one who shaved Slade's heads. 'Harry Hair,' as the band nicknamed him, was based in London's Soho, and by the time he had finished with them they looked like new recruits in the army. Don and Noddy liked the look, but Dave absolutely hated it. It was a miracle Chandler was able to convince him to get his hair cut in the first place. But he knew that for Dave Hill money was a big motivating force and he used this to get his own way, Noddy commented, 'All he had to say to Dave was, "Davey, you'll be a millionaire if you have this done."' But although the ploy worked, the guitar player still wasn't keen. Many years later Noddy would reveal in a TV interview, 'Dave hated [the skinhead days] with a vengeance.'

Ben Sherman shirts, turned-up jeans held up with braces and big Doc Martin 'bovver' boots were purchased, and finally the look was complete. As soon as photographs began to appear in the press the band realized Chandler was right. With no other bands dressing anything like this, they certainly grabbed people's attention.

Jimi Hendrix shared manager Chas Chandler with Slade, and also their barber.

AND THEN THEY WERE SLADE

'There was a new skinhead band around, and they had bigger stacks of amps, and they were louder than we were. And we didn't like that!'

Rick Parfitt, Status Quo

It was Chas Chandler who took the bold step of shortening the band's name simply to Slade. He had never liked it and he felt, quite rightly, that the new name was catchier and much more easy to remember. The boys were fine with this change because they had never been that keen on the name in the first place.

Slade's hard new look grabbed the attention of the media before long a controversy blew up. The general public was shocked, and the question of violence and football gangs was raised. There was

Left: Shock tactics. Slade get tough.

concern that Slade would infect Britain's youth, already out of control and fighting on the terraces every Saturday afternoon at football matches. But the band got the attention they so badly needed. As Holder confirms, 'It was a shock tactic... it got our foot in the door... and that was the object of the exercise, really.'

Family and friends were indeed shocked by the new image. Don said, 'When my Mum waved me off, I had hair down to here [points to shoulder], and when I came back I was a skinhead. The next morning she brought a cup of tea in and poured it all over me 'cos she thought someone else was in

The football hooligan look wouldn't last long.

look as just a fashion, to others it was a way of life. Walking down any high street in Britain you would see young men dressed in the same way. Slade simply utilised the look and put it on a stage; they were never really hooligans. With no knowledge of their previous incarnation as The 'N Betweens, the press and fans in London thought they really *were* football hooligans.

Dave Hill wasn't comfortable with the hard man image at all. He had always dressed flamboyantly, and even went as far to wear a dress on stage when they were in the Bahamas. But now, things were different. 'We were always playing darts in the dressing room – we didn't dare go out the front in case we got beaten up,' he admits. But not everyone in the band felt so intimidated. Although Jim was uneasy looking like a football thug, Noddy and Don, who were real working-class boys, liked looking tough. There was another positive point to all this, too: promoters no longer felt they could mess them around and they all paid up immediately!

Although there was a lot of interest in the band and reviews of their music were positive, inevitably the band began to attract a skinhead following – and these young men were the real deal. Don remembers, 'We played in Bournemouth one night, and it was full of skinheads, and oh my God, we were on stage, and they just saw right through us.' Dave adds, 'We weren't quite right because we had a violin player, and they were into reggae.' And the image had a downside. 'We couldn't get on *Top Of The Pops* because the producer's son had been beaten up by skinheads,' recalls Dave, bitterly. Although the situation would eventually change, already it was an indication that the skinhead look could turn out to be a problem.

Now there was tension at the gigs and a threat of violence present. This wasn't what the band was about at all. They were a party band and they wanted people to have fun. But now they had 'bovver boys' hanging around and the atmosphere had changed. The band took to carrying an air rifle in the van. Although it was never loaded, after one gig in Guildford they were forced to threaten a gang of

the bed!' Their loyal local following didn't care for the look either, and audiences pleaded for them to grow their hair back as soon as possible. Other bands on the local circuit who knew them well were also perturbed by their aggressive new image, but one thing was for sure, everyone now knew exactly who they were. Slade looked hard, and the other bands were scared of them. Even though they were still the same four lads from the Midlands, things had changed. Chandler's extremely unpopular idea of a skinhead look was working. The powerful sound of the band playing live and the tough guy image was an impressive combination.

With skinheads, there was always a threat of violence. Although many regarded the skinhead skinheads with it. In his autobiography Noddy tells the story: 'We threw the ... equipment into the back of the van, jumped in and locked the doors. I grabbed the rifle, wound the window down and pretended I was about to shoot them. You've never seen a gang of skinheads scarper so fast in your life. It was comical. They were running in all directions, screaming.' Noddy was not one to be easily intimidated and he and the boys had had lots of experience of rough audiences in the clubs up and down Britain and also during their time out in Germany. 'The skin audience wasn't that rough. If I look back at some of the pubs I played in the Black Country when they were pissed up and Saturday night was fighting night, then skinheads weren't too bad.'

Noddy had such a casual manner on stage that he could win over even the most hostile of audiences. But the bad-boy following was not what the band wanted. Their change of image had certainly attracted attention, but now that it had started to work against them, perhaps it was time for another change.

Chandler brought the boys a new song written by songwriters Winsley and Saker entitled 'Wild Winds Are Blowing'. He thought it would be ideal for the band and although they wanted to write their own songs, they went along with it because Chandler said it would be good for them. So far, he had been right, so who were they to argue?

'Wild Winds Are Blowing' was the first song Slade ever recorded with Chandler, and it was released in 1969 as a single on the Polydor label. Chandler had released all of Jimi Hendrix's records with Polydor and he felt more comfortable with the staff. As Polydor was still under the Philips' umbrella, it was an easy and obvious switch for him to make.

Slade made their very first TV appearance on *The Alan Price Show* in late 1969. Chandler and Price had been in the Animals together (Price was the keyboard player), and they remained friends. On leaving the group he had had some solo hits that included 'Simon Smith and His Amazing Dancing Bear'. As well as their new single Slade also performed a cover of The Beatles' song 'Martha My Dear' featuring the multi-instrumentalist Jim Lea on electric violin. Dave Hill also talked to the audience and introduced the songs. Watching this early TV

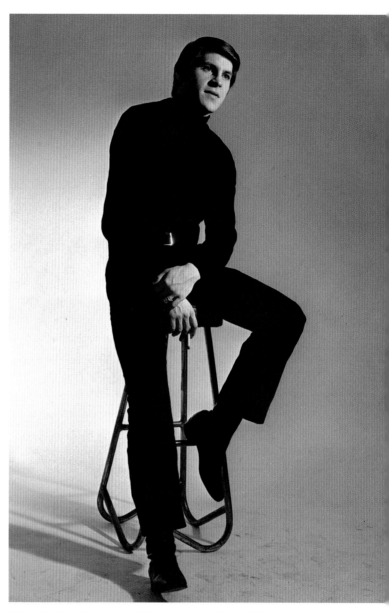

Alan Price. Keyboard player, vocalist with The Animals and friend of Chas Chandler.

show is a reminder of just how young the band really was; they were just boys. They were also very different to anything else that was around at the time: the music, the instruments they used, the look – not to mention Noddy's skull-crushing voice.

The band went down well and they thoroughly enjoyed their TV debut, especially guitar player Dave, who basked in all the attention. It would be the first of many TV appearances for Slade, whose time, it seemed, had really come at last.

Slade's next television appearance was on the

BBC's *Top Of The Pops* to promote their follow-up single 'The Shape Of Things To Come', originally recorded by Max Frost And The Troopers and the theme tune to a movie called *Wild In The Streets*. This was the first song the group ever played on *Top Of The Pops* and they were understandably nervous about this particular performance. It was now 1970 and *Top Of The Pops* was the all-important music show in Britain. It felt like proof that they were finally making some kind of headway. After all, if you were on *Top Of The Pops*, you were famous.

'The Shape Of Things To Come' was the first song the group ever performed on *Top Of The Pops*, and they were understandably nervous. Yet they remained characteristically cocky. "I remember when we first went on *Top of the Pops*,' says Jim Lea. 'The scenery was all held together with tape, and it wasn't that wonderful ball you see on TV, and such is the arrogance of youth that I thought: we can take this.'

Also appearing was a singer-songwriter at a piano: the young Elton John was making his *TOTP* debut performing 'Lady Samantha'. He was in the very early stages of his career and was trying to get ahead, just like Slade. Later he would adopt a glam style, but the fashion would serve more as a disguise. Dave Hill, who was stuck with cropped hair and bovver boots, was jealous of Elton John's flamboyant clothes. 'He was afraid Elton would pull all the girls,' says Noddy. 'How wrong can you be?'

Not long after their barnstorming performance on *Top of the Pops,* Slade went in to record at the famous Olympic Studios in mid-1970 where many of the big bands of the day recorded their music. They were excited at the prospect of being in the place where The Rolling Stones and The Who had recorded, not to mention Hendrix, who Chandler had worked with there. They were booked into a new, smaller studio that had just been built, and spent three weeks working on what would become their next album, *Play It Loud*. Chandler wanted the band to write for the album and like them, he was convinced they could produce a hit. Dave and Noddy teamed up, as did Don and Jim. They asked Chandler for advice on song writing and Noddy remembers his response well. 'You're a gutsy rock'n'roll band, so write gutsy rock'n'roll songs,' he said. Although they worked hard

nothing much came of it at first. Ever-sensitive to their needs, Chandler reassured them, saying that Hendrix hadn't become famous just because of his talent: it was down to hard work. The band kept at it, writing and discarding, and then writing some more. All the while, Chandler educated and encouraged them, bolstering their growing confidence in themselves as recording artists. This was so different to anything they had experienced before. It was the real thing: here they were in a big-time studio with a big-time producer who had absolute faith in them. To a man, the boys were determined to repay that faith.

Play It Loud

In November 1970 Slade released *Play It Loud* on Polydor records. It was their first album under the name Slade, and was the product of their first proper studio recordings. All in all it's a rather serious affair, earnest and almost bleak. This is reflected in the stark black-and-white cover featuring Noddy sporting a big flat cap and the boys with their hair grown out of their crop style, looking scruffy in drainpipe jeans. They were moving away from the heavy, hard image, yet some TV shows and magazines were reluctant to feature Slade. The whole package had an austere feel and there wasn't much to signal that this was, in actual fact, a party band.

Jam-packed with musical ideas, *Play It Loud* is musically quite a long way off from where Slade would eventually end up. The drums are dry, with no hint of the echo-like stomps and clapping for which Slade would later become so famous. The guitar sounds are primitive and raw, the riffs are simple but effective, yet the vocal sound demands attention.

The opening track, the jerky 'Raven', has a performance from Noddy that somehow calls Bob Dylan to mind; it includes the ironic lyric from the future kings of glam, 'all that glitters is not gold'. The sparse arrangements give the material a flat feel,

Right: The young singer-songwriter Elton John.

Slade slowly softened their skinhead image, which had begun to work against them.

and sonically it's more brittle than brutal, but it's tough nonetheless.

Written by Jim and Don, 'Dapple Rose' is a thoughtful ballad featuring a piano. The pair were also behind 'I Remember', which features some particularly prophetic lyrics from Don:

> *My kids said hello and I didn't reply, you see my memory was gone*
> *Like a fire in the grass it just wiped out my past and my memory's gone...*

Don was later to lose his memory after a horrific road accident in 1973. 'I don't remember what the inspiration was,' he says, 'but that is very weird! I must be more careful in the future about what I write.'

Elsewhere, proto-type Metal riffs appear sporadically, and Dave gets a little funky on 'Dirty Joker' with some basic WahWah guitar work. 'Joker' also includes some tasty bass moves from Jimmy in a decidedly John

Entwistle style. The sexually suggestive 'Sweet Box' features a tribal drum section and the lyric, 'Put me in your sweet box'. And it's not the only instance of *double entendre* to be found in Noddy's lyrics: 'My Friend Stan' takes on a completely different connotation when listened to from this suggestive angle.

All the other self-penned tunes are composed by Lee, Holder and Powell. Hill only contributes to one song, 'Know Who You Are'. There's a conscience at work here, and lyrically a shadow of social comment:

> *Maybe you're wrong, finding a new way out*
> *Trying to work out a way to include one another...*
> *Think what you are, think where you're going to!*

Although it was released as a single, 'Know Who You Are' failed to chart.

Play It Loud is the sound of a young band experimenting and stretching themselves. With no formula yet in place for them to follow, and no

The ephemeral T. Rex whose single, 'Ride A White Swan', had caught Noddy's ear.

pressure to write a hit, the band could just relax and play. Even though not all the songs work and some of the ideas miss the mark, there's an innocence there and a willingness to take chances that the band would back away from later on.

Referred to by music journalist Charles Shaar Murray – the legendary music journalist who started his career at *OZ* magazine and who went on to work at the *NME* – as 'the great forgotten Slade album', *Play It Loud* was a fine debut – but it still didn't give them a hit record. Although the band was bitterly disappointed, Chandler wasn't worried. He knew they had the potential to be successful: all they needed was the right song and they would be off and running. The boys, on the other hand, were really frustrated. To them, it seemed as if all they ever had was one false start after another. It was hard on them; though they believed in themselves wholeheartedly, they were getting impatient. They had been slogging away for five years now, and they still couldn't get a hit.

'It was just a matter of having the luck to have the right record at the right time to get the breaks, and that was the only thing we ever doubted,' says Noddy. 'We always had amazing confidence in ourselves. We had no doubt in our minds that we would break through at some point. And that when we did break through it would snowball for us.'

After one late-night gig at the Temple Club in Wardour Street, London, in 1970, the club DJ was playing a new record that really caught Noddy's attention. He asked the DJ who it was, and 'T. Rex,' came the reply. 'Ride A White Swan' was doing well in the pop chart, and Noddy knew straight away that this song was somehow special, important even. Of course, he was right.

Picked up by Atlantic's American subsidiary, Cotillion, *Play It Loud* did nothing in the USA. But it received mostly good reviews in the UK, and the group's popularity was growing. Despite the lack of a hit Slade were selling out at bigger venues than many of the chart bands with hit singles. They were gaining a dedicated following, earning good money and they remained optimistic. Privately, they felt that the skinhead look was definitely working against them, and it was time to move on to a brighter image. Once that was in place, all they would need would be that breakthrough record.

GET DOWN AND GET WITH IT

'It's all down to having a good time. It's partying music.'

Dave Hill

For some two years, Slade's set had always ended with a cover of a song made famous by Little Richard: 'Get Down and Get With It'. A wild, bluesy rocker that the band ripped up every night, it always went down a storm and the audiences loved it. At Noddy's behest all the skins would stamp their feet in time with the beat. The floor would shake and the atmosphere was like a circus with Noddy as the ringmaster, just the way he liked it. This was the centrepiece of their live concerts and really showcased the band's power, not to mention Noddy's phenomenal voice. 'The first time we played this on stage, the reaction was so fantastic we knew it had to be a single,' says Noddy. Chas Chandler told the band they needed to capture

on tape the same vibe they produced on stage and so they both decided to release the Little Richard cover as the next single. Once they had come up with the idea, it seemed so obvious.

It's a common misconception that Little Richard wrote 'Get Down And Get With It'. In fact, it was Bobby Marchan. Born in 1930, in the 1950s he had been the vocalist for Huey 'Piano' Smith and the Clowns, going on to find fame with his 1960 R&B chart-topper 'There Is Something On Your Mind'. Slade simply assumed Little Richard had written the song, and were threatened with a lawsuit when the song's publisher, The Burlington Music Company, discovered that they had had a UK hit with Marchan's song. Eventually, however, the suit was dropped.

Slade recorded 'Get Down And Get With It' at the Olympic studios. To capture that 'live' vibe,

Left: Let the Glam begin.

they turned everything up as loud as possible and powered through the song as if they were in front of an audience. 'It was the first time we had laid down the vocals and backing at the same time to capture the feel,' Noddy recalls.

Today modern recording techniques see singers doing take after take, the best of which are compiled into one definitive vocal. There is also the extensive use of auto-tuners and all the options digital recording offers. But Slade laid the whole track down 'live', and that was basically the finished record. They got it in one magical take, and Noddy's vocal was retained almost in its entirety.

Chas Chandler built his recordings around the vocal, which, in his opinion, was as the most important element in a pop record. Everything was sacrificed to the voice and nothing was allowed to interfere with the message it carried. However, in his autobiography Noddy recalls that this time, Chas felt there was something missing from the track – and so it was. They needed the foot-stomping sound the crowd supplied at live shows.

The band set out to find a solution. At the studio an echoing stairwell was found and the band stamped and clapped their way through layer upon layer of multiple-tracked takes. The end result was perfect, sounding as if 100 fans were having a party in the studio. They had achieved their goal of capturing their live sound on tape.

With this record, the vibe was there, the raucous power was there: it encapsulated the whole Slade sound. Dave Hill said that 'Get Down' was 'all about atmosphere', and he was right – it had tons of the stuff. Everyone was excited: could 'Get Down And Get With It' be the hit that would finally break them?

'Get Down And Get With It' was released in June 1971, and the pioneer broadcaster John Peel immediately picked up on the single. While he championed it, many radio DJs refused to play the song because they felt it was too rowdy. However, the single sold solidly and consistently, and the band watched themselves go slowly up the charts. It was the group's very first hit record and it reached a

Slade 'rock out' on TV.

respectable No. 16 in the UK charts.

At this time, Union rules meant that there had to be a certain amount of live music on the radio, and the lads benefited from this, playing *The Radio 1 Club*, which was recorded live. The record was played on the radio all the time, and finally the band felt as if they were actually getting somewhere. They would feel a tremendous sense of achievement every time they heard the song on the airwaves, calling each other up to say, 'We're on again!'

Once again Slade appeared on *Top Of The Pops*, this time, in November 1971, as a hit group, and for the first time ever they had girls screaming at them. Dave Hill loved it. Never a 'teeny' band, they were used to a more male-oriented audience but they liked the new group of female fans that had adopted them. This was a proper hit and all their hard work had really paid off. After all the false starts and disappointments, they now had something to celebrate. Noddy wrote in his autobiography, 'It was our first real taste of success, our foot was in the door of fame.'

But the hard work had only just begun. If the band thought they had put in some hard graft up until now, this would prove to be nothing compared to what was to come. And if they thought that this success made them impervious to further disappointment or tragedy, they would have to think again. They were on the crest of a wave and success was on its way to make all their dreams come true, but at what cost?

But for now, Slade were enjoying their hard-earned success. Phil Symes of *Disc* magazine called them 'probably the most entertaining live band around,' while Deborah Thomas declared in the *Daily Mirror* newspaper, 'There's no doubt that Slade are the most exciting group to erupt on the pop scene this year.' But there was one dissenting voice in the shape of Mike Guy, writing in the rock bible that is the Burnham-On-Sea *Gazette*: 'The outfit may be one of the most popular acts on the circuit right now, but I found their amplification intolerably loud.'

Slade's image was finally moving away from the skinhead style. Not only was their hair getting longer, their clothes were also becoming bolder and brighter. Their legendary glam look was

starting to emerge.

In July 1971, with one hit single under their belts, Slade were set to play on a bandstand in the centre of a lake in Amsterdam's Vondelpark. But Chas Chandler was unhappy because for about 30 per cent of the audience a large tree was cutting out the view of the stage. 'Tell the promoter to get rid of that tree!' he screamed at an interpreter in the thickest of Geordie

Slade wait to be introduced on 'Top of the Pops' by 1970s' Radio 1 DJ, Noel Edmonds.

accents. 'Tell him if he doesn't cut down the tree, I'll throw him in the lake and cut it down myself!' The tree was promptly cut down. Back at the hotel later that evening, after Slade turned in an incredible set to an audience who could see everything from all angles,

Chandler explained why it was so important. 'It's all about being seen. You can be the best band in the world but if nobody can see, you might as well be the worst. *You have to be seen.*' The physically imposing Chandler always made sure his band could be seen.

Chandler didn't want Slade to record another cover. He felt that this time it had to be an original composition, and he was convinced they could do it. But the group themselves weren't so sure. Previous writing sessions had excited them, but produced precious little. The band had always wanted to write their own songs but their lack of success in coming up with something they all felt was really special had dented their confidence. No one was particularly optimistic at the prospect of writing new material, but Chandler managed to convince them that if they really wanted longevity it was the only way forward. 'We didn't consider ourselves that strong as writers,' says Noddy, 'but he said "you've got the talent to be good writers, particularly you and Jimmy". And he pushed us in that direction. He said, "You must start writing, you must write, write, write!"'

'Coz I Luv You'

Jim and Noddy got together and began experimenting with a riff they had had for ages. For years they had played it on sound checks and they decided this was as good a place to start as any. Jim Lea remembers, 'I took my violin and went over and knocked on Nod's door. His mum made a cup of cocoa, and I said, "I've got this idea, this rhythm, and it's a shuffle." Half an hour later the cocoa was drunk and "Coz I Luv You" was born, just like that.'

They elaborated on the basic theme, wrote a chord progression and played around with the rhythm some more. Noddy decided to go for it and started singing off the top of his head, and by the time the two had finished, no more than half an hour later, they had a song. This was their first serious, focused effort to write a hit single and it paid off. In a documentary *Slade*, shown on the BBC over Christmas in 1999 and hosted by Slade fan Mark Radcliffe, Noddy commented, 'It was the first time we'd actually, me and Jim, sat down to write a song properly together.' They just knew it was good.

When the lads played Chas Chandler their new song, they were a little nervous because the manager could be brutally frank. When they had finished there was a moment's pause before Chandler said, 'I think you have just written your first Number 1.' Jim and Noddy thought he was joking, but he couldn't have been more serious. In that moment they all realised the situation had changed: if they really could write material of that calibre, then anything was possible.

The basic construction of 'Coz' was simple. The arrangement was direct and the tune catchy. Slade recorded it in two days and used similar musical moves to those on 'Get Down'. There was the same stamping and clapping, but for Noddy's vocal chants, 'Hey, Hey, Hey' replaced 'Yeah, Yeah, Yeah.' Dave cranked out the riff and Don kicked the beat out of the drums relentlessly. The whole of Noddy's vocal take was recorded with the band as a run-through, but it was so good they patched up a few words and kept nearly all of the original performance. Chandler recorded everything when the band was in the studio and he especially liked to catch the singer's many spontaneous ad-libs, which would often become integral parts of the songs.

Slade's live sound had always had an extra dimension – Jimmy's violin. When the band played live, bass-playing duties would be passed to Dave or Noddy if Jim was required on violin or piano. On 'Coz I Luv You', Jim's violin playing was heavily featured, an instrument that at that time wasn't often heard in pop music – and if it was, had certainly never sounded like this.

There was an ethereal quality to 'Coz I Luv You' that really caught the ear. According to Noddy, once they put the clapping sounds on the track (once again recorded in a corridor at the studio), 'the song came alive.' It all worked tremendously well, but when the band had finished recording and mixing they were shocked to discover they didn't like the song that much. They felt it was too 'poppy', simply not as powerful and heavy as 'Get Down And Get With It'. Chas Chandler, however, loved it.

Noddy said 'Because I Love You' looked too 'soppy' when written down. The band hated the way the title looked; it didn't suit their image. Noddy came up with the novel idea of writing it on the sleeve in the same way as graffiti was scrawled on

walls back home in the Midlands: 'COZ I LUV YOU'.
Drummer Don recalls, 'In the Midlands that was
the frenetic way of writing at the time, and that's
where that came from.' Don adds that they were
trying to 'heavy things up' with this style of writing.
It all contributed to their rock'n'roll, rebellious vibe.
'Write it how you say it – I always wrote my lyrics
like that anyway… it became our trademark,' says
Noddy. Slade wanted the whole thing to look as
tough as the music sounded.

Released in October 1971, the song was
constantly played on the radio. The DJs loved it, and
the record became an immediate turntable hit. Radio
coverage turned into sales and a staggering 500,000
copies were sold in two weeks. 'Coz I Luv You' was
massive. In no time at all, the single reached No. 2
and once again the band was invited to play on the
hugely influential *Top Of The Pops*. Rod Stewart was
at No. 1 with his evergreen classic 'Maggie May',
which was set to stay in the top slot for a long time.
No one was going to knock the hugely successful Rod
off the coveted No. 1 slot... or would they?

The First of Many

Just a week later, Slade was back in the *Top Of The
Pops* studio as the No. 1 act. The young Black Country
upstarts had knocked the mighty Stewart off his perch.
Noddy recalls in his autobiography that the band drove
to London in silence. They were all so excited they just
didn't know what to say to each other. He thought to
himself, 'Oh my God, we've knocked Rod Stewart off
the top of the charts!'

Slade arrived at the *TOTP* studios to find that
their record company had filled their dressing
room with Champagne, and they invited all the
other artists on the show to help them celebrate.
This was the first of many times at the BBC
when they would conduct an open house policy
and encourage all to join in the fun. They were
everybody's best friends. In 2002 Noddy Holder
would tell John Robb, 'Our dressing room on *Top
Of The Pops* was party central. That was where all

*Rocker Rod Stewart. Slade knocked his classic
'Maggie May' off the No. 1 spot.*

the booze was! The Sweet we knew pretty well and I still see Andy Scott, Mott [The Hoople], Mud… Les Gray [of Mud] liked a drink! Suzie Quatro… Bolan, we knew him even though we were meant to be rivals but we would have a good chat, he was a real nice bloke.'

Everyone enjoyed Slade's hospitality, though Marc Bolan was quoted as saying that Slade were no real competition to him. Jim Lea took this to heart saying, 'I never forgave him for that!' Little did the T Rex front man realise just how much Slade were to be his future rivals. By the time Slade were in full flight, having hit after hit, Bolan's career was faltering.

Slade were thrilled to appear on national

Left: All Glammed Up. Slade enjoy their success.
Below: Suzi Quatro. The undisputed Queen of Glam.

television as the No. 1 pop group in the country. Dave Hill strutted for all he was worth, loving every minute of it. Noddy's cheeky grin was permanently fixed in place as Don chewed gum and pounded the hell out of the kit. Jim smiled knowingly to himself and threw shapes. They were all fantastic front men. Noddy and Dave immediately grabbed people's attention with their undoubted charisma, but Jim was also a dynamic performer who gave 100 per cent in all his TV and stage performances. He would put his foot up on Don's drum kit and throw himself across the stage. He really knew how to project; he was a vibrant, vital ingredient to Slade's energy on stage. His bass playing was fluid and imaginative, and his song-writing skills exemplary. Don would sit steadfast, chewing gum, looking handsome while smashing the beat out of the drums with a ferocious power. Dave Hill said Don was an 'immense' drummer and he was right. Never flash or over-the-top, Powell kept it simple and laid down the beat relentlessly. Imaginative and tasteful, his playing never overshadowing the music, he always played for the song. Like every great band, it was all about chemistry.

It was the first time Slade wore big platform shoes and outrageous, colourful outfits. At the time glam rock didn't exist, but the lads had always liked loud and lively clothes. Left to their own devices they would always gravitate toward the brighter end of the fashion spectrum. They loved the garish, the over-the-top, the ridiculous even.

Slade were working-class lads made good and they wanted to drain every last drop of fun out of the situation. They didn't want to play at being big stars with attitudes to match. This was a laugh; this was thrilling. They were determined to have a ball. It was a feeling almost of relief that something had finally happened. The hard work had indeed paid off, they were No. 1 and, as Noddy would later comment, 'When you're *Top Of The Pops*, it's the best feeling in the world!'

However, Slade didn't have it all their own way, as music journalist Charles Shaar Murray remembers. He first saw them live around this time when they performed at the Lanchester Arts Festival, 'They'd just made No. 1 with "Coz I Luv You", and the vast

majority of the assembled company were only dimly aware of them. "Weren't they that bunch of losers who used to pretend to be [choke] skinheads?" Anyway, they came as close to dying the death as they've probably ever come. Noddy Holder compounded the felony by trying to bully the audience into responding. They did their set and split. To say that they left without trailing clouds of glory is something of an understatement.'

Nonetheless Slade were building up a huge, loyal following of dedicated British fans. 'It was our first taste of screaming girl fans,' remembers Noddy. 'God knows why we got screamers in, we weren't the prettiest band going by any stretch of the imagination!' They were hardly a pin-up band but that's what they became. Suzi Quatro didn't think any of them were heart-throbs, but 'Don was the best looking,' she says. The band's fame was already wasted on Jim, who had already begun to dislike the attention, but for now they were the four happiest guys on the planet.

The band never really thought about 'career moves', leaving all of that to Chandler. They had worked hard for their success but were philosophical about the situation. At the time Noddy commented, 'I'd rather do something that makes me happy. If it only lasts five years, I'll know I've done what I wanted to do, and if I've shit it up, then it's purely my own fault and nobody else's.'

Success with their very first song together galvanised the writing partnership of Holder and Lea. It was to prove to be an extremely prolific and successful team that would produce a five-year run of constant hit singles. Noddy says, 'That gave us fantastic confidence. Once we'd written a hit, and it became a No. 1 record we thought, well, we can do it! It was at that point that we became writers as much as anything else.' The writing partnership of Holder and Lea would become the basis of the band's whole career.

Almost overnight their lives had changed. 'Hysteria breaks out at their stage appearances,' declared David Wigg at the *Daily Express*, while the

Right: Marc Bolan, always one of Slade's biggest rivals.

New Musical Express said, 'Bands like Slade are proving that audiences want to rave.' Even Charles Shaar Murray began to revise his opinion, writing in the *NME*, 'What dance-hall yobbo could resist it?' Slade were on the front cover of all the pop magazines, and were recognised everywhere they went. The teen publications that had previously shunned them now welcomed them with open arms. The media simply couldn't get enough of Slade. It was what the boys in the band had always dreamed of.

Slade gigs were now even wilder than before. They had been pre-booked to play their normal size venues, but the success of 'Coz I Luv You' sent them into the stratosphere. The small clubs and theatres were swamped with new fans. People were queuing up the street to get in, desperate for a glimpse of the band they'd seen on television. It was pure madness. The band travelled to Europe in the winter of 1971 to promote the single, where it was a huge hit in many countries, including Germany and Scandinavia. They did a few gigs, but mostly it was an endless parade of TV shows and photo sessions. Like it or not, the boys were pop stars.

But despite their hit record there was one problem: there was nothing to follow up 'Coz I Luv You'. Ever the ideas man, Chas Chandler thought it would be a good for the band to record a live album. This was a strange move so early in the group's career, but they needed a stop-gap. They had to keep the momentum going; a live record could be recorded quickly and might just give them the time they needed to write more material without disappearing off the pop radar – for good.

Left: Slade, backstage, ready to rock.
Below: The Glam Rock kings.

IT'S ALIVE

5

'When Slade broke in 1972 I began to get really nervous. Here I am killing myself to write the next incredible riff and then I see these four blokes pounding out four chords over and over, and loving every minute of it. I bought all of their albums and thought, maybe I wanted to join the band. Bands like Slade really inspired me to get back to my root of inspiration: heavy, intelligent but fun rock and roll.'

Ritchie Blackmore, Deep Purple

The group agreed that an in-concert album would be ideal and in November 1971 three nights were booked at a large studio just off London's Piccadilly Circus. As the studio usually catered for large orchestras, it was big enough to hold a Slade audience. The band planned on playing the Tuesday, Wednesday and Thursday nights, choosing the best versions of each song over the three evenings. Free gigs were announced on the radio and through

Left: The band 'ham it up' for the cameras with Dave centre stage, of course.

the fan club, and in consequence, every night was packed to the rafters.

On the Wednesday night the band had come straight from the *Top Of The Pops* studios, where they had just recorded another performance of the single 'Coz I Luv You' for transmission on the Thursday evening. The record was in its third week at No. 1, and morale was at an all-time high. The atmosphere was palpable, and everyone agreed that the Wednesday night recording was by far the best. All the songs they recorded that night would go on to be used on *Slade Alive!*

These days, live recordings are culled from whole tours, with each track specially chosen and then digitally corrected over a period of months. In contrast, *Slade Alive!* was recorded in one night with no changes or re-recordings, with the whole project – three nights' recording and mixing the album – was completed in less than a week. Apart from a few vocal over-dubs from Noddy, this was as live as it got. This was a *real* live record!

In a gesture typical of the band's ethos, Chas Chandler had the idea to run a competition in *The Sun* newspaper for a fan to design the album's sleeve. It worked perfectly; the band was seen as all-round good guys, which of course they were. Not only did the winner get to design the sleeve for their favourite group's new album, he or she also got the chance to travel with them on their first trip to the USA. There were thousands of entries, and the band was thrilled with the response. The winning design featured two teddy bears, one big and one small, and was featured on the inside of the gatefold sleeve; the cover itself featured a shot of the band on stage. There is no record of any fan flying out to the States with them.

Slade Alive! was released by Polydor in March 1972 and went straight to No. 1. It would be nearly ten years before another live album would reach the top of the charts, when heavy metal band Motorhead's *No Sleep Til' Hammersmith* made it to the top spot in the summer of 1981.

Only seven songs appear, which is rare; an in-concert recording would usually include over 12 songs and span two discs, which in the Seventies this could sometimes be stretched to three. But as ever, Slade showed restraint and simply presented the best songs of the evening. The album starts with the mean, hard blues of Alvin Lee's 'Hear Me Calling'; it chugs along menacingly only to explode into a glorious power riff extravaganza. Don really goes for it – triplets all over the kit with an incessant crash ride cymbal. The pounding outro reveals Slade's belligerent rock attitude; this is tough, rock-hard stuff, and not what you would expect if all you had heard were the hits. Dave Hill's guitar bristles with a true blues authenticity as it growls and moans.

The vocal harmonies are thick, high and focused with elements that both Sweet and Queen were to borrow from liberally later on. Noddy shows how delicate he can be on the rock ballad 'Darling Be Home Soon' written by John Benson Sebastian, made famous by The Loving Spoonful in 1967 and also covered by The Association and Joe Cocker. Here, the quality of his voice really shines through, proving he doesn't always have to use his 'screamer' mode to make an impact. Noddy's notorious burp in the middle of the quiet sensitive section became a staple that was expected every night. The song is sentimental and he couldn't resist sending it up. The infamous belch was a combination of beer and mischief.

Slade Alive! includes a truly electrifying version of their earlier single release 'Know Who You Are', which improves upon the studio recording included on 'Play It Loud'. Their self-penned 'Keep On Rocking' is a nod to their early rock'n'roll heroes Chuck Berry and Little Richard. Noddy's voice sounds like a chainsaw ripping through concrete; here and on 'Get Down And Get With It' his vocal is positively superhuman, and it's remarkable that he was able to sing like this night after night. Both of these songs show the band at their boogie-woogie party best. Don dictates the pace, holding the whole thing down with apparent ease, and Jim supplies rock'n'roll bass runs that Led Zeppelin's John Paul Jones might be proud of. The band takes the audience through various singalongs before finishing in style with a cover of Steppenwolf's rock classic 'Born To Be Wild'; Dave's guitar is abrasive, with a rock'n'roll swagger that demonstrates his confidence, the white noise solo is reminiscent of Jimmy Page and that distinctive wah-wah pedal sound will be used to great effect later that decade on Sweet's No. 1 hit 'Blockbuster'. All in all, it's a tour-de-force of rock'n'roll mayhem.

As Noddy told *Melody Maker*, 'The beat is the main thing with us. We like to hit their guts with the beat and get some feeling going through their bloodstream into their hands. If you want to come and sit down, and delve into the music, it's no good coming to see us. I think we could play like that if we wanted to, but we don't want to. We get our kicks from pulsating music.' For a while *Slade Alive!* would secure the boys' desire to be taken seriously as an 'albums' band, rather than just a pop group that released catchy singles. They wanted to compete with big bands like The Who, Deep Purple and Led Zeppelin. The live album was definitely a huge step in that direction. It was another reason why the record didn't include the obvious hit singles, and it worked. People who had previously ignored Slade were now taking notice of them.

Everything Slade were about as a band was captured on *Slade Alive!* It stayed in the UK album chart for an amazing 18 months, and to this day it remains the favourite album of many fans. For anyone unfamiliar with Slade's music, this is a great starting point.

But the time not everyone felt the same. In October 1972 'Metal' Mike Saunders wrote in *Phonograph Record*, 'In short, *Slade Alive!* isn't merely mediocre, it's awful. It's rock and roll, sure, but as much as I hate to admit it, there is such a thing as bad R&R. Some groups just don't have it, and despite their status as one of England's biggest hard rock groups, that's about where Slade stand on this album.' However, in the same publication Greg Shaw wrote, 'This is one of the best live albums I've ever heard. Mike Saunders is out of his mind... I can't get enough of this album.' Jon Tiven of *Rolling Stone* said, 'This is the genuine thing from start to finish', but perhaps Lester Bangs said it best; 'What *Slade Alive!* is, is gut-bust concrete sledgehammer get-it-off-junk-jive for right now!'

The skinhead image faded long ago, but now the band had grown their hair and returned to wearing colourful clothes – especially Dave Hill. Their whole look had moved from what Don describes as 'the skinhead period, grey shirts, boots et cetera' to 'the *Star Wars* bar!' The skinhead image was indeed ancient history and it seemed as though it belonged to another era, almost to another band.

With the release of the live album the lads had bought themselves some time to write new material, and their next song turned out to be 'Look Wot You

Dave Hill sparkles and shines, all dressed up to the nines.

Dun'. With a hard, thumping beat, it was written on a piano, and although it wasn't as raucous as previous Slade recordings, it still reached No. 2 in the UK charts. At the time the band didn't rate the song that much, but it definitely stood the test of time and became a classic track.

'Look Wot You Dun' was released three weeks after 'Coz' dropped out of the British chart. The band embarked on a promotional tour of the UK and Europe, where they appeared on TV show after TV show, and smiled for the cameras until their faces ached. They even met and made friends with fellow chart-toppers (and musical rivals). Everybody liked the Black Country boys, and they were having a fantastic time.

Slade Hit the Road

The band now embarked on their first bona fide tour since their massive hit records. They moved up into big theatres and halls, and tickets sold out everywhere. Their image was developing and they hunted for more and more outrageous clothes. They began wearing pink jackets and tartan flat caps, anything, as long as it was colourful. Noddy even grew his sideburns.

The reaction to the group was incredible; people were talking about how they hadn't seen the like since Beatlemania. Everywhere they went there was madness and mayhem. At times, the situation was out of control, but the lads fed off the attention. They were having a whale of a time.

The support act on the tour was none other than Status Quo. 'We couldn't believe it, we'd been ruling the roost and all of a sudden they came along, and we were supporting them, says Rick Parfitt. 'I don't know how that happened, but the combination of the two bands in one night was great for the audience.' Dave Hill says, 'They were a serious group, y'know, you had to be on the case when you followed Quo.' The fans were a mix of young

Left: The boys 'Keep On Rockin'!

Denim-clad rockers Status Quo.

lads who were into bands like The Who and Led
Zeppelin, and a barrage of screaming girls who were
pure pop fans.

After their first show in Glasgow, Noddy was
nearly arrested for saying the F-word on stage. He
had always used bad language when he performed.
It had never mattered before, but now there were
young kids in the audience and some parents
complained. Police came to the band's dressing
room, where everyone was drinking and enjoying
the back-stage arrangements. Although Chas
Chandler was scared they were going to drag him off
to the local station and charge him, Noddy was let
off with a caution.

The tour was a resounding success; at long last the
band had really arrived. There were sold-out shows,
screaming fans outside their five-star hotels and a
huge road crew who looked after their every need.
It was all a far cry from the small pubs and run down

guesthouses of the Black Country, and those long,
cold journeys in their old van. They were famous and
things would never be the same.

Jim Lea disliked the attention but was
philosophical about it all. 'We don't have time for
any superstar image. We feel we are just like the
audience,' he said at the time. Dave Hill would go out
and talk to the screaming girls; he loved being known
by everyone and thrived on being at the centre of
things. 'We don't mind mixing with our fans, whereas
most groups usually get to the stage where they don't
even talk to 'em,' he said.

It's often said that getting to the top is easy, but
but staying there is tough. Slade knew this, and they
realised they needed another hit song – and fast. The
tour was over, they were a huge success, but the ball
had to be kept rolling. Jim and Noddy got together to
write some new material.

The next single Slade released was 'Take Me Bak

'Ome'. The idea came from all the travelling they had done in the early days. Jim Lea explains, 'We used to just get in the van and drive home; we'd drive through the night just to get home.' 'Take Me Bak 'Ome' was recorded as a deliberate exercise to show what Slade sounded like live. The group felt that their previous two singles hadn't properly represented their live show, but this one certainly did.

The song moved slowly up the charts. No one could understand what was happening. How could this not be a hit? Until now everything had been going so well for them, and the new track was typical rowdy Slade, so what on earth could be the problem? The band was nervous. They didn't want things to fall apart as quickly as they had come together for them.

The Lincoln Festival

While the single crawled up the hit parade the band were invited to play the Lincoln Festival. This was a hip, four-day affair that would run over the May bank holiday – also on the bill was Genesis, Humble Pie, Rory Gallagher, Roxy Music, Don McClean, Joe Cocker and The Beach Boys. Legendary screen villain Stanley Baker, who was a huge music fan and a Slade fan to boot, arranged it all. The band accepted the invitation and joined the bill that included such bands as The Beach Boys, Status Quo and Rod Stewart and the Faces. Most surprisingly the comedy team Monty Python's Flying Circus were also on the bill and not only that, Chas Chandler had pushed for Slade to follow them. The band was furious when they found out, but Chandler knew what he was doing. He realised that after sitting through Monty Python the crowd would be ready for anything; the Pythons, though extremely funny, would test any rock audience's patience after an hour or so. He was correct.

It was a rainy evening, and by the time the lads were due to hit the stage the crowd were wet and hungry for some music. The Python team left the stage, but when Slade came on it was to a chorus of boos. Bass player Jimmy remembers, 'We played the Lincoln Festival, it was raining and we were booed on!' This had never happened before, but then this was a trendy audience with all the fashionable journalists at the front just ready to bury what they considered to be the latest, lightweight pop phenomenon. 'They thought, what's this band doing here?' explains Noddy. 'I thought, we'll show you bastards.' As darkness fell the stage lights came up, signalling the audience to rise to their feet. 'After the first number they were all up on their feet!' says Noddy. Slade were a party band – they always had been – and they really knew how to get a crowd on their side. Everybody's best mate, Noddy charmed everyone he performed in front of. The band was at their best; brash, loud and irreverent. The audience didn't stand a chance.

In a magazine interview in February 1972 Noddy commented, 'If they come along feeling down, we try and send them away smiling.' That's exactly what happened at the Lincoln festival. 'It gave us this credibility as a great rock live act,' Noddy continued, 'and the next week "Take Me Back Home" went to No. 1 in the charts as well.'

Slade were a huge success at the festival and they felt their performance cemented their position alongside all those so-called 'credible' acts. The following week they appeared on the front cover of every music paper and magazine. Many of them ran a picture of Noddy in a bowler hat with a badge on the front that read 'The Pope Smokes Dope'.

Once again the band felt justified: here they were, back at No. 1 in the UK chart. Chandler had always insisted that the band release a single immediately on the back of the previous one and this technique was working. At this point they were hardly ever out of the UK charts and although at the time there were many good bands around, no one could touch Slade – they were in a class of their own.

At this point in 1972 glam rock didn't really exist. The only other glam contender was Marc Bolan of T. Rex, the band that had impressed Noddy so much a few years earlier. In 1971 T. Rex had had a huge hit with 'Get It On'. Marc Bolan wore wear glitter tears on his face. Dave Hill loved this look and would soon follow suit, taking the thing to a whole new level.

Noddy and the boys were always on the lookout for new, striking clothes. Don Powell took to wearing stripes. Everything would be striped – trousers, shirt, waistcoat, even his shoes. Noddy started to have suits specially made with huge checks in garish colours. Jim was the more soberly dressed of the group. He would wear jackets with sparkles on, slight platforms, and that was it. But Dave Hill was a completely different animal and made it a personal crusade to be as flamboyant as possible. Dave had always loved dressing up, and now he was presented with the perfect excuse and the ultimate platform from which to indulge his most outrageous sartorial notions.

Dave went completely over the top with the glam look. His platform shoes got higher and higher and in the end he became positively dangerous. One night in Liverpool, the band were rushed off stage due to a fan invasion and, in the chaos, Dave fell off his massive platform shoes. This particular pair sported a big $ sign down the side and were his highest ever. Dave broke his leg and for the next few gigs played in a wheelchair, with Noddy taking great pleasure in pushing the guitar player around the stage.

Below: Slade celebrate backstage.
Right: The constantly over-the-top Dave Hill goes for it and the baco foil covers a multitude of sins.

'MAMA WEER ALL CRAZEE NOW'

'They were a proper geezer's band, but they dressed like the Diddy Men, didn't they?'
Noel Gallagher, Oasis

Things were going brilliantly, but success came at a price. The pressure on Noddy Holder and Jim Lea to come up with yet another hit song was relentless. They had to keep on coming up with fresh ideas and each new tune had to be as good, if not better, than the last. Everyone, Chas Chandler, the rest of the band, the record company and fans were constantly waiting for the next Slade hit.

In the late summer of 1972 Jim and Noddy wrote a song called 'My, My, We're All Crazy Now.' Its title was inspired by the way Noddy felt at the Lincoln Festival as he looked around and saw everyone going wild. The pair worked on the song and by the time they were finished they knew it was a potential single.

Left: Right on! Slade in all their sartorial elegance.

Back in the studio Noddy and Jim played their new song for Chas on acoustic guitars. He loved it, and said that 'Mama Weer All Crazee Now' was 'Brilliant.' The boys immediately picked him up on the fact that he had misheard the song's title, but as soon as they said this they knew Chas's title was much better. The title stayed as Chas had heard it, and the boys knew that this song was good – possibly the best they had written so far. Once again they were tremendously excited about their new composition, but there was also a sense of relief that they had once again come up with something good enough to be a potential hit. The pressure was off, but only for the time being. They knew that within a month or so everyone would be expecting yet another hit.

'Mama' was a rip-roaring affair. It was the perfect Slade single – raucous, rowdy and catchy. The band

Ms Quatro, a stalwart of the era. Suzi would sometimes swap her de rigueur leather-clad look for a more Glam approach.

really enjoyed performing the song live because it was so much fun to play. and this came across on the recording. Noddy did his usual ad-libs, which producer Chandler picked up on immediately. He kept the singer's warm-up howl at the start of the song and made the chant Holder came up with the centrepiece of the record's fade-out. The band already had a trademark sound but here it was perfected. 'Mama' was the ultimate blueprint for a rockin' Slade single.

With two No. 1 records under their belt the band were flying high, and it seemed as if they could do no wrong. With the release of their next single they would have to do something remarkable. Once again they had to keep things moving forward, to keep up the pressure and push themselves to the next level. Chas Chandler decided that 'Mama Weer All Crazee Now' would have to enter the chart at No. 1. This was pretty much unheard of and had only happened five times since the charts began back in the Fifties. Chandler and the record company started to devise a plan whereby the band could fulfill this tough demand.

Slade previewed the song on *Top Of The Pops* and the record was played on the radio relentlessly. Despite this, 'Mama Weer All Crazee Now' entered the UK chart at No. 2. The problem was that on the week of release the band had to fly to America and weren't available to do the much-needed press interviews and promotion that would have just given the single that final push. The timing was wrong, and this was one of the few times when Chandler made a mistake. But the US was waiting for Slade and the time was right to tour there. It was a catch-22 situation: stay and promote 'Mama' or tour the States.

The following week the new single reached No. 1 without the band being in the country and they instinctively knew that next time they could go straight in at No. 1. 'Mama' was an enormous success, and the music business all started to look to Slade as the new leaders in pop. They may not have captured the zeitgeist, but they were wiping the floor with every other pop act in the business. They seemed unstoppable.

It was around this time that glam Rock began to emerge and soon lots of bands started to adopt Slade's look. Groups like Mud, Sweet and Gary Glitter came along, and the glam fashion helped their careers. From just Slade and T. Rex, suddenly there were all sorts of bands jumping on the glam bandwagon,

Mud in full 'Glam' regalia.

Above: The Blockbusting Glam Rock outfit, Sweet.

and before long there was out-and-out competition to see who could out-glam the other. Slade stomped where Bolan preened and when Marc whispered Noddy screamed. Mud joked, Slade grabbed you by the throat! Sweet harmonised, Noddy and the boys terrorised, but one thing's for sure: they *all* liked to dress up.

Dave went further and further with his flamboyant outfits. Jim found it extremely frustrating. He wanted the music to speak for itself and felt that Dave's get-ups and antics were turning the band into a joke, which in a way it was; they even took to giving Dave's outfits names such as 'The Metal Nun' and 'Foghorn Leghorn'. But although they got lots of attention from

Dave's clothes and behaviour, Jim felt it detracted from the music.

But there was no stopping Dave. He would get dressed in the toilets at the studios of *Top Of The Pops,* and it wasn't until he came out that the rest of the band would see exactly how ridiculous he looked this time. 'Come on, H, reveal!' Noddy would call, from outside the cubicle.

Dave's outrageousness was working and the band were having massive hits, but Jim felt there would

Right: The boots that 'weren't' made for walking. Dave in his dangerous dollar sign platforms.

be a price to pay for all this frivolity. Along with Noddy, Jim was the songwriter and he took what he did very seriously. He felt the whole thing was being devalued by this ridiculous posturing. Slade's singles were huge hits, but was the dressing up getting out of hand? Would there indeed be a penalty to be paid somewhere down the line?

Getting Slayed in the USA

The band travelled to the USA for the first time in late August 1972. Their records had been released in the US but there had been no success. To make any impression on the American public and music business alike, you simply had to be there. Slade were signed to Polydor records who were hardly a rock'n'roll label. Their two biggest acts at this point in time were the R&B singer and inventor of funk, James Brown, and German composer and band leader James Last.

On their arrival in the States, Polydor supplied a bus for crew and equipment, and two limos for the band. But, not realising that the limos were actually for them, the boys simply piled into the bus and sped off. However, it wouldn't take long for them to realise how differently things were done on this side of the pond.

The band was booked into LA's infamous Hyatt Hotel, nicknamed 'The Riot House' because of all the debauchery that was rumoured to take place there. A second home for fellow Black Country boys Led Zeppelin, it was here that Slade had their first experience of LA groupies, who offered themselves to the band as they explored the various bars on Sunset Strip. Dave Hill told an American music journalist, 'We're not the biggest bunch of ravers, but we do know what we like. We don't overstep our limits. Groupies… I love them, they're funny kids. They make the scene, and it's always fascinating to meet them.'

A picture of Noddy dressed in the mirrored top hat that had by now become his trademark was on a massive billboard on the Strip. Their single was at No. 1 back home, and the band was on top of the world; they really felt they had arrived. Here they were in America, hanging out with rock stars like Alice Cooper. He would say of the band, 'Slade was the coolest band in England.' Their every need was catered for, the band were having a ball. It was amazing.

Their American manager, Peter Kauf, was a friend of Chas Chandler from Hendrix days. He suggested Slade play small clubs and let the whole thing grow naturally. But Chandler disagreed. He was used to his artists being stars and he wanted them treated accordingly. He should have listened to Kauf, who knew his own territory – but he didn't. Chandler saw Slade as 'his' band and he wasn't about to take advice from anyone else. Consequently, Polydor made the big mistake of hailing the band as the 'new Beatles', which was the kiss of death. Jim Lea protested, 'The most common comparison they make is to the Beatles which is ridiculous.' In Noddy's book *Who's Crazee Now?*, he recalls, 'We didn't want to be seen as the new Beatles. When the British press had said that about us, we had always replied, "We're not the new Beatles, we're the first Slade." That was our stock line. Over there, we couldn't get away with that.'

The band had little or no following in the States, and they were shocked at the lack of interest. In Britain they couldn't walk down the street without being hassled to the point of riot, but in America they would walk on stage to polite applause. Holder told music journalist Greg Shaw, 'We've got to start all over again in America, playin' the bottom of the bill, gettin' the audience to know the songs and that. It's just like startin' all over again'.

Slade were booked on a three-week tour to support British supergroup Humble Pie, featuring Stevie Marriot from The Small Faces and Peter Frampton from The Herd. On their first night with Humble Pie they played a huge indoor arena in San Diego. They went down OK but they didn't cause the crazy, uncontrollable audience reaction they were used to back in Britain. Eventually, they realised the whole audience was stoned. Smoking

Hear me calling! Noddy 'works' the audience.

*Above: All wrapped up in the Stars and Stripes.
Slade salute America.*

marijuana at gigs was commonplace in America, especially in Seventies California, and this partly explained the audience's lack-lustre response. Noddy stood at the side of the stage and watched the masterful Steve Marriot at work with this zonked-out crowd. He was a consummate professional and Noddy soon learned that dealing with stoned Americans was very different to entertaining excited British pop fans.

Used to long guitar solos and big stadium anthems, the Humble Pie audiences were confused by their rowdy rock, pop tunes. Slade went on and cranked out their comparatively concise songs, one after the other, but they just didn't ignite the American crowds in the same way as they did back home. The band never bombed; they adjusted to

Right: Noddy and his outrageous 'Kipper Tie'.

The band with their lead singer in top hat and tartan.

playing the big arenas and always managed to gain favour, but their look and sound just didn't slot in with the current trends. Sometimes the 'Pie' audience would get bored of Slade. 'We came in for a bit of stick from some Pie supporters during our only slow number, "Be Home Soon"', recalls Noddy. 'I just said, "Look, if you want to see Pie they'll be on soon, so why don't you just go out for a crap while we're on?" It's crude, but it works because it breaks the ice.'

But American audiences remained bemused by the group's outrageously flamboyant clothes. They worse too-short tartan trousers with yellow socks, braces, stacked boots and silver overcoats; they wore purple jackets, girly chokers, bright yellow suits and a whole array of top hats. Slade were quintessentially British. Irreverent and wacky, there was an eccentric edge to the band but their wit and charm seemed lost on American audiences. They couldn't relate to the band's lack of sophistication, but that was Slade's strength: they were a no-nonsense bunch who rocked. The Americans were mostly puzzled. Slowly, however, they were gaining fans – often from the more industrial areas of the United States.

During the tour of America Slade had to fly home for an unavoidable, previously booked one-off gig in a theatre called The Sundown in London. The band flew from California to London, played the show and immediately flew back to California.

Audiences may not have known what to make of them, but there were those in the US music press who liked what they saw. In November 1972 Greg Shaw wrote in *Phonograph Record*, 'In a flash the lights are thrown on and you're hit by a great gut-churning, toe-tingling wall of sound. The drumbeats thunder as if shot from cannons; the high-pitched guitars wail like the cries of a thousand banshees. LOUD is the word of the day.' He described them as 'strangely reminiscent of Alex and his three loathesome droogs of *Clockwork Orange* fame. Certainly none of the four qualify as your average run-of-the-mill, nattily dressed English pop star sex symbol... Vocalist Noddy Holder is downright ugly, outfitted in a pair of baggy multi-coloured pants, suspenders and a reflector-speckled top hat. Lead guitarist Dave Hill is a real eye-catcher as well, decked out in his skin-tight silver suit and cape with matching 4"-heeled boots. Only bassist Jimmy Lea and drummer Don Powell keep up anywhere near a normal appearance, both totally engrossed in pounding away at their instruments.' He comes to the conclusion that Slade are, 'the rawest, crudest, ravingest group to invade American soil since Black Sabbath.'

Slade returned to Britain in September 1972 after three weeks on the road. They had made an impression on young rock fans in the States, but they were hardly stars. Back in the UK, the pressure of supplying yet another hit record returned. 'Mama Weer All Crazee Now' had fallen out of the charts and, although it was a massive hit for them, the record company demanded another.

GLAMTASTIC

'Slade was certainly our greatest influence; not only in the crafting of rock songs but also as performers. Before Slade, no one really knew shit about how to make an audience riot. We really got off on that. There would probably never have been us without them.'

Gene Simmons, Kiss

'Gudbuy 'T Jane' was written right at the end of a recording session in late 1972. The group's time had nearly run out and they were using up the last half-hour. Jim and Noddy had the bare bones of a song, so producer Chas Chandler suggested they get it down on tape for future reference. They laid the backing track down fast, while Noddy wrote the lyric. It sounded great; the next day some overdubs were done and the song was finished. Chandler told the band that this would

Left: Gene Simmons on stage with Kiss. Glam Rock, American style.

be the next single. In no time at all and almost by accident the band had written another hit.

The 'Jane' in question was a young girl the band encountered on a TV show in the States. She was a co-presenter, although according to Noddy's autobiography she never said a word; she just sat there looking pretty. Just before they went on air, she had caused a big fuss because she couldn't find her special shoes, or, as she called them, her 'Forties Trip Boots'. The whole scenario had stuck in Noddy's mind and inspired him to write a song. Jim came up with the title, changing it from Noddy's original 'Hello 'T Jane' to 'Gudbuy 'T Jane'.

Left: Slade give it maximum Glam Slam for the TV cameras.

In November 1972 the single was released, and it was an instant classic. It seemed that the band could do no wrong, although the top slot eluded them this time, with 'Gudbuy 'T Jane' only reaching No. 2 on the UK chart. There was the endless round of photo sessions and interviews, while Dave and the lads continued to parade about on the stages of *Top Of The Pops* and other TV studios across Europe in their outlandish costumes.

Les Grey, lead singer with fellow glam band Mud, says, 'We didn't wake up one morning dressed in silver and high boots looking like we'd been beamed down from Mars; it wasn't like that! Well, you'd be

Above: Noddy in his crowning glory, the iconic mirrored hat.
Left: Brian Eno of art rock Glam band Roxy Music.

forgiven thinking Dave [Hill] had been.' Charles Shaar Murray observed, 'While the likes of Bowie and Eno [Roxy Music] looked weird for specific reasons, Dancing Dave looked weird just for the hell of it.'

Two major glam items that Slade gave to the world became truly iconic. First, there was Noddy's top hat. He had covered the hat with mirrors himself after seeing Lulu on stage wearing a dress that had mirrors attached. The hat's mirrors would catch the light, reflecting it out over the audience. As a direct result of touring with Slade and seeing Noddy with his mirrored top hat, Phil Lynott of Thin Lizzy would go on to use a mirrored scratch plate on his bass guitar. As Noddy says, 'It became a symbol of the glam rock years.'

Second on the list was Dave Hill's 'Super Yob'

Above: Even the enigmatic David Bowie climbed aboard the Glam bandwagon for a while.
Left: 'Super Yob' Dave Hill. He wanted something 'space aged' and boy did he get it!

guitar, a silver, Space Age-shaped instrument designed by John Birch. Throughout the Seventies Dave used 'Super Yob' on hundreds of TV shows and it was an important part of his look. Eventually he had several more 'Yob' guitars made in various colours, including Black and Sunburst, but the most enduring model was the silver version, now owned by Adam and the Ants guitar player Marco Pirroni.

Slade's outfits were truly glamtastic, but now plenty of other artists were joining in with the fashion. The ethereal, other worldly David Bowie was in full flight with his iconic creation 'Ziggy Stardust'.

He had performed the single 'Starman' on *Top Of The Pops* and, although he exercised a little more reserve and had better taste than the Slade boys, he too was wearing make-up and glitter. Jim Lea's frustration remained, but the band were having so much fun with their new-found fame and success that for the time being his unease was allayed. Of Hill's sartorial excursions, he said, 'Dave was on the planet Zog where this was concerned.' Dave, however, was hamming it up and loving the attention. 'You write 'em and I'll sell 'em!', he'd say.

Slayed?

In December 1972 the band released their second album of the year. *Slayed?* was their first studio record in two years, and it went straight to No. 1 in the UK. *Slayed?* featured their hit singles 'Gudbuy T'Jane' and 'Mama Weer All Crazee Now' plus the b-side 'I Won't Let it 'Appen Again' plus some brand new songs. This album was where the Slade formula was blueprinted. All the trademarks appear – the often ignored, clandestine vocal harmonies, Dave's signature guitar tricks and Don's snare drum patterns, all of which helped to give Slade's records their very particular sound.

Jim's melodies and arrangements are smooth and natural, with the songs sounding almost as though they have written themselves. Jim's bass playing is solid yet languid, flowing smoothly but digging in hard where necessary. Noddy's lyrics are as cocky as ever, but there are numerous thoughtful moments too, for instance 'Look At Last Nite', about the fickle world of showbusiness and the 'here today, gone tomorrow' nature of the pop industry. You could almost call it the blue print for The Jam's 'To Be Someone'.

Noddy sounds incredible on *Slayed?*, at turns like both John Lennon and Robert Plant. There is an almost reserved element to his delivery at times, something that makes you want to listen to him even more than when he is in full-on scream mode for song after song. But that's not to say he's

The lads in all their glory.

doesn't spend much of the album roaring at the top of his lungs, and 'Gudbuy, Gudbuy' finds him well and truly on top vocal form.

After recording Janis Joplin's 'Move Over' on a BBC Radio session in the summer of 1972, the band had decided to re-record it for the album. Joplin is obviously an influence on Holder, Jim's bass playing is lithe and expressive, and the whole band sound at their dynamic best. The No. 2 hit 'Gudbuy 'T Jane' makes an appearance, as does the No. 1 single, 'Mama Weer All Crazee Now'. *Slayed?* is a complete pop and rock package, and should be a part of any true rock fan's collection. With an album like this the band could expect to rival some of the best rock talent out there, but, somewhat unfairly, their massive single sales were putting off some of the more discerning rock fans.

There was by now a growing sense of rivalry between T. Rex and Slade. It was mostly media-driven, but many fans and journalists joined in. As Noddy

explained to one American journalist, 'The thing is, it's because T. Rex came up as a big group in England, a really massive group in England, where they had two or three hits before we ever got a hit. Then we come up and started gettin' our Number Ones in a row, so people tagged us as their biggest competitors.' Warming to his subject, he continued, 'People have called us competitors, but with T. Rex it's just a one-man group. Bolan and three backin' musicians. With us it's a four-man group. In England everybody knows Marc Bolan, but not many people know the other three in the band, except for the real ardent fans, and that's a true shame because there's absolutely no individual identity to relate to. There's only Marc Bolan, and hence, he's T. Rex. In England all four of us are known as well as one another. Everybody takes an equal part in the group.' He concluded, 'Bolan has sort of a star quality on stage and he's not touchable… Bolan's appeal is mainly to a girl's audience; he gets the screamers at his shows and all that. With us, we get an equal number of girls and

Above: The 20th Century Boy, Marc Bolan.
Right: Suzi Quatro. The Glam Queen learned a lot
from watching Noddy on stage.

singer Phil Lynot at the side of the stage watching him and learning in much the same way as he had done with Steve Marriot from Humble Pie. He had a wonderful talent for making everyone in the audience feel like his best friend, a skill Phil Lynott would eventually hone for himself. Suzi would also stand at the side of the stage every night with her boyfriend, soon-to-be-husband and future Slade 2 manager, Len Tuckey. As she later commented in a television interview, 'It was a nice little learning curve for me.'

The Tour was sold out and the madness that surrounded Slade escalated. The band were playing better than ever and the audience reaction was incredible. The group played the world famous

fellas at our shows, more fellas than girls, maybe. And it's not the scream scene at all. It's the join-in chantin' and shoutin', and football slogans and all that bit, you know. So we're miles apart in that respect.'

Chas Chadler put the band back out on the road in November 1972 with two support acts, the unknown Suzi Quatro, a young leather-clad female singer and bass player from Detroit, brought over from the States by pop mogul Mickey Most. Before producer and RAK record label owner Most plucked Suzi from obscurity, she was in a band with her sisters called The Pleasureseekers. They were regulars on the local Detroit gig circuit in the late '60s and they would sometimes open for shock rocker Alice Cooper. Suzi was in awe of Slade. In an interview for the television programme Glam Night on Britain's Channel Four, she says of the band, 'I always thought they were just very loud. That's how I remember them: loud! *Very loud*!'

Also on the bill was Thin Lizzy, a three-piece rock outfit from Ireland. Still very much in their formative years, to date their only hit had been the folky sounding 'Whiskey In The Jar'. Quatro, who had little experience at this level, and the Lizzy boys, who were still finding their feet, would learn much from the already seasoned pros Slade. Noddy said that he would spot Lizzy lead

London Palladium, at that time the home of light entertainment in Britain. The venue had never hosted a rock show before. Noddy asked for the orchestra pit to be cleared of instruments, but he was ignored. Mid-way through the show the Palladium's management called the fire brigade because the balcony was physically moving up and down. The audience had jumped into the orchestra pit and chaos ensued. Slade were banned from every Stoll Moss venue in the country.

The group's fans would often get so raucous it would end in destruction. Wrote rock journalist Lester Bangs wrote after a show in Liverpool, 'I peered down through the curtain and there, in front of the empty stage, was a curious mound almost six feet high. It was composed of the remains of all the chairs in the first two rows. The audience had stomped and broken them into tiny pieces, then piled them up in a monument to Slade.'

Despite this, the band enjoyed a close relationship with their fans. 'We're a workin' class band, workin' class kids,' says Noddy. 'With us, the audience is part of the band. The music is just 50 per cent of Slade. The dressing up and the humour and the audience involvement is the other 50 per cent.' Charles Shaar Murray wrote in the *New Musical Express*, 'They *were* that audience. They weren't leaders; they were just four cats who had everything in common with the people they were playing to. They weren't aiming at them, or even playing to them; they were just naturally part of them.'

Despite this, the situation was getting out of hand and although it pained the band, they had to put a barrier between themselves and their fans. They began to have police escorts in and out of the shows, and would use decoys to get back into their hotels. Still the fans would camp outside and sing Slade songs all night. They took pains to stay out of sight; if the fans saw them, there would be bedlam. Although the band were excited by all this insanity, it did take its toll. Their lives were no longer their own, it was difficult for friends to come back stage to see them and they had to hide away in their hotel suites. Their home town became their only place of solace: everywhere else, they were public property. Now Slade were seriously famous, and

there was no escaping it.

Thin Lizzy accompanied Slade on their next tour of America – which started almost directly after the UK tour – and the bands became firm friends. They were a powerful rock'n'roll band who, it's rumoured, were once asked to leave a Queen tour because they were too good. Phil Lynott was an impressive frontman, someone who in a later interview even Noddy would call 'a bit of a madman.' The archetypal wild rocker, he lived the lifestyle to the full; indeed, he would later be forced to leave the tour after contracting hepatitis.

This time around the band knew what to expect in America and took the whole US experience a little more in their stride. With the usual round of TV studios, interviews, gigs, planes and tour madness, the schedule was gruelling, but the lads handled it. 'You should see the schedule!' complained Jimmy Lea at the time. 'We go to Los Angeles tomorrow. In two days it's one radio station after another, and interviews galore.' Noddy remarked, 'We've done a couple of small clubs and packed in a couple of thousand, and it was just like the old Marquee days. We did two in Ohio, for example, and they were solid, a real gas.'

The band was attracting a more enthusiastic audience now, and Dave told US music journalist Barbera Charone, 'We can do a lot for the morale of music here. It needs a kick, something fresh and new… We're just connected with pure entertainment.' Noddy gave his usual orders to the crowd to get up and dance, telling them to clap and stamp their feet. Meanwhile, the ushers would step in to make the kids sit down. Noddy would yell, 'Leave them alone… we're just trying to have a good time!' At least one of their old problems had been solved: as Dave Hill observed, 'The druggies seem to be thinning out. They can't get off on anything – they just sit there.'

The band liked America and it was vitally important to all of them that they conquered it. As Dave said, 'The States is the last place we have to make it; then we'll just do world tours… God knows when we'll stop – it's a case of getting as big as we possibly can.' He continued excitedly, 'The Who have grown up now… they're older. But Slade are *now*! To hell with the old… I know what we've got and it's a damn sight better than anything else. Most bands

Phil Lynot. Lead singer and front man of the Irish rock band Thin Lizzy.

don't have any personality, and kids'll get off on anything that gives them a good time.'

Cum On, Let's Go Straight To No. 1

After one of the US shows, Noddy was surprised by the audience's enthusiastic response; it was almost like being back in Britain. He kept on thinking back to the show and how much power he felt from the audience. Later he wrote some lyrics entitled 'Come On Hear The Noise'. But although he liked what he'd written, it still didn't quite sum up the way he felt. That was the key; he'd really *felt* the noise that night. He changed the song title to 'Cum On Feel The Noize'. 'We'd done a gig where the audience was just rattling the walls, amazing volume, and to get over our volume was even more

amazing,' he says. 'So this one night they were shouting so hard you could actually feel it in your chest, and so I came up with "Cum On Feel The Noize."' Classic Slade, this was arguably their finest song-writing moment.

Slade began playing 'Cum On Feel The Noize' live a long time before it was released as a single, and it always went down well. This was unusual; once a band becomes successful the fans often only want to hear the hits. 'Cum On Feel The Noize' was an exception and the crowds loved it.

Meanwhile, Chas Chandler was still obsessed with the group going straight in to the UK charts at No. 1. The last band to do it was The Beatles, and he was determined that Slade should equal them. They had come so close, but still hadn't managed it. Chandler pulled every trick in the book to make it happen, but you could never be 100 per cent sure. Today 5,000 sales can easily get you into the top 30; Slade had a staggering, almost unbelievable 500,000 pre-orders for 'Noize'. It was a huge amount of sales, even for the Seventies, but still not an absolute guarantee of the top spot.

But 'Cum On Feel The Noize' went straight in at No. 1. They had done it. Their glam rival Marc Bolan had released '20th Century Boy', but Slade held Bolan off, keeping him at bay at No. 2. It was a major moment in their career, catapulting them into a whole new arena of fame.

Young girls in the audience now began throwing their underwear at the boys on stage. Noddy quipped, 'I wouldn't clean my guitar with anything else.' He would shout, 'Hands up all the girls in the audience with black knickers on… Hands up all the girls with red knickers on… Hands up all the girls with no knickers on!' The place would go berserk.

Slade were constantly on TV in full glam regalia, Noddy wearing his 'Jack-The-Lad' suits while Don chewed gum and looked cool, his drumsticks bound with coloured tape. Dave Hill was now more outrageous than any other glam star and had taken to wearing silver suits and overcoats. He told journalist John Ingham, 'I've always liked science fiction, and I've always thought it would be great to wear a spacesuit. Then about 13 months ago I came across this silver leather, so I had a whole costume designed. I put glitter on my face and hair to sort of balance it out.' Jim would grin constantly and bounce around the stage, occasionally glancing at Dave in disbelief.

Slade became ubiquitous; there was no escaping their seeming omnipresence. But if they thought things had been crazy before, they had seen nothing yet. Slade were down-to-earth boys, who loved to make music. For them, the joy was the playing, not the fame. But there was a bubble closing in around the band the more successful they became. This can be fatal, and in many cases groups find their life becomes lived through the public's perception of what they think the group are. They see themselves reflected in magazines and on TV screens, and somehow that image becomes a reality to them. Slowly the real band members can somehow disappear. This detachment can destroy personalities as the ego becomes overblown and out of control from all the adulation. If the situation escalates, it can lead to a band imploding or an individual becoming a megalomaniac.

Slade had worked so hard and come so far that

hey weren't about to succumb to this, but the danger was there. To their credit, they hung onto a reality many others had long since lost and simply enjoyed their amazing ride. Their time had come and they were making the most of it. The band enjoyed their success but unlike many of their contemporaries, they never used drugs. Cocaine was the drug of rock stars but they never touched the stuff. Ozzy Osbourne once commented, 'I hope they got the sex, the drugs and the rock'n'roll – they are fools if they didn't.' Years later Noddy said, 'We weren't a druggy band; we were a boozing band. One of the reasons was because we saw too many fatalities amongst our mates that were doing it. I mean, they were dropping like flies in the 1970s. We were, in a way, too professional to go that same way. We never partied until the job was done. When we were doing an album, or be it a gig or whatever, we were always on the money; we were always very focused on what we wanted at the end of the day. And then we'd go overboard afterwards. But we certainly weren't going to let the partying be the main part of our life. The partying came after the work was finished.'

Slade Mania In Australia

In the first few months of 1973 the band headed out to Australia. Slade's records had been big hits, and Chandler was keen to capitalise on the success the group had already had there. The tour was a package affair with Caravan, the Newcastle-based band Lindisfarne and their old friends Status Quo. Slade, of course, were the headline act; Quo were always great fun and Lindisfarne were all up for a party, especially lead singer-songwriter Alan Hull, whose capacity for drinking was legendary. They knew they would have a fantastic time on the road with all their mates.

Until they arrived the band had no idea just how big they were in Australia. Dave said, 'In fact we were at No. 1, 2 and No. 3 [in the singles chart], a bit like The Beatles really.' He recalled people saying, 'You've

Geordie band Lindisfarne support Slade in Australia.

had all these hits like The Beatles did. When are you going to do Sgt Pepper?' 'Unfortunately we haven't got songs about pilchards climbing up the Eiffel Tower,' he would reply. They were just as successful in Australia as they were back in Britain, and it freaked them out that they could be so famous in a place they had never been to before. They started to realise just what international success really meant.

From Australia they flew straight to Japan, where they had a wild old time in the bars, clubs and discos. They liked the Japanese women and made the most of the opportunities that came their way. Their records had been reasonably successful out there, but that wasn't really important to them. They were yet again amazed to see that people knew who they were in such a far-off, exotic place.

Who knows what the Japanese made of Dave Hill's increasingly bizarre stage outfits and Noddy all decked out like the Mad Hatter at his own tea party? That's anyone's guess. Just like Britain, however, the audiences went crazy at the shows and there were

nightly riots. At the time there was a law in Japan forbidding anyone to stand up at gigs, but Noddy was having none of it, and every night he encouraged the audience to get up and have a good time. The authorities were not amused, but no one ever got hurt. They just enjoyed themselves, and that's what Slade were all about.

Slade were making pop history. They felt they could conquer the world and as far as singles were concerned they had no rival, but on the album front other bands were pulling ahead. Slade ignored this, feeling it was something that could easily be addressed. They were shifting an immense amount of singles and every venue they played around the world was a sell-out; they weren't worried. The band were all still in their early twenties and they felt they had plenty of time to achieve their goals.

The band travelled back to the States on a regular basis, where their popularity grew. In September 1973 they changed record companies and signed to Warner Brothers. It was unbelievable that a good-time band like Slade had not had a single hit record in the United States, and Warner were determined to change all that. Noddy declared, 'A hit would certainly help – so far the most we have managed was to make No. 60 in the charts with "Gudbye T' Jane." But "Cum On Feel The Noize" seems to be going well now, and that could be the one.'

For this latest US tour all kinds of bands were brought forward as support acts, from Santana to King Crimson and The Strawbs to Iggy Pop, and Slade were included on some bizarre bills. Iggy was going through a particularly tough time with drugs and would be carted off to hospital at regular intervals. The wild-card singer had his own opinion of the boys from the Black Country. He once said in an interview, 'I wouldn't call them the best dressed band I've ever seen, but boy they could

rock! I said to my manager, "Y'know dude, they can kick some fuckin' ass, and they're a bunch of badly dressed limeys!'

Slade played festival after festival, sharing the bill with bands and artists such as Sly and the Family Stone, Steeley Dan, Motown legend Stevie Wonder and Lou Reed. One night they came across an up-and-coming group of country rockers called The Eagles. Don Powell stood at the side of the stage and was shocked at how good they were, asking, 'Who are these guys?'. They would go on to become his favourite group.

According to Noddy's autobiography, Kiss saw the band's New York show, and they readily admit that their own style and philosophy came from listening to and watching Slade. The next day *The New York Times* griped, 'To think Britain sent us The Beatles, and now they send us THIS.'

The Sensational Alex Harvey Band.

Skweeze Me, Pleeze Me

The pace was quickening and the band were in the middle of a roller-coaster ride that seemed never-ending, always offering new highs. In June 1973 they unleashed their new single 'Skweeze Me, Pleeze Me' on an expectant British record-buying public. Amazingly, it went straight in at No. 1 and for them it was the ultimate doubly whammy. Doing it once was thrilling enough, but twice seemed almost beyond comprehension. Chas Chandler had worked the same magic as he did on 'Noize', and it worked beautifully.

Slade had always been confident about their abilities and now that confidence had been rewarded. On their summer tour of Britain, Slade pulled into Blackburn, a grey-looking cotton town in Lancashire. The venue was King George's Hall right in the centre, its 2,200 seats sold out long before Slade arrived in town. By the time they arrived 'Skweeze Me, Pleeze Me' was No. 1 in the charts. The support band was The Sensational Alex Harvey Band – ironically, a group Slade had previously supported on their sojourns to Scotland – and that night they delivered a truly stunning set. Lead singer Alex poured a bottle of Guinness over his head to slick back his hair, and delivered an amazing version of the Tom Jones hit 'Delilah' as an encore. Harvey and his band were on top form and it took 20 minutes for the applause to die down. It was a response to daunt even the most confident band.

Half an hour or so later Slade came on stage, decked out in their outrageous *Top of the Pops* outfits. Noddy took centre stage, pulled the microphone down to waist level, let out an almighty fart and roared, 'Good evening Blackburn, how does it smell?' Once again the irrepressible showman, who never feared an audience or another band, won the audience over; and the support act was all but forgotten. The lads were on top of the world.

SMASHES, CRASHES AND ROCKIN' THE MASSES

8

'There's more to be learned about the nature of class warfare from a Slade gig than from just about any other current cultural event.'

Charles Shaar Murray, NME, September 1973

On this, their biggest ever tour, Slade were booked to play the huge arena at Earls Court. Today it's a regular rock venue, but in July 1973 no other band had played there before, and they were set to make history. Unfortunately, glam star David Bowie beat them to it. Although he booked shows there after Slade, his dates came

before so he stole their thunder. But the show was sold out and 'Skweeze' was still top of the charts.

This was the pinnacle of their success so far and the gig was absolute mayhem. There were 18,000 fans, all dressed in full glam regalia, and Slade took the roof off the place. Noddy played with the audience and drew trick after trick from his showman's armoury. Dave Hill struck pose after pose as Jim laughed, threw shapes and put his foot

Left: Rockin' up a storm in 1973.

The greatest songwriters of their generation,
Holder and Lea.

up on Don's bass drum. The drummer chewed gum, grinned for all he was worth and pounded thunderbolt beats out of his kit ferociously.

Slade had become, without question, the biggest live act in Britain, and Earls Court was a testament to Slade's success so far. It was a grand glam ceremony; as Noddy recalls, 'There were loads of top hats with mirrors and silver-clad Dave look-alikes.' Dave adds, 'What I've heard from fans since is that you should have been in the Tube – it was glitter, top hats...'

The gig had been was a huge celebration between band and fans, the climax of an already amazing career, and the boys were astonished by their success. All their dreams had come true; they were the kings of the glam generation. Success was exhilarating, and they felt invincible. Surely nothing could take this feeling away from them.

It was a quiet evening in July 1973 and Don Powell took his gleaming white Bentley out to collect his girlfriend, Angela Morris, from the nightclub in Wolverhampton where she worked. On the journey home, Don lost control of the car, hit a wall and the couple were thrown through the windscreen. Angela was killed instantly; she was just 20 years old. Don survived, but with horrific injuries. He was rushed to hospital where the doctors gave him 24 hours to live. The rest of the lads were notified, and rushed to his bedside.

Don was in a terrible state, with cuts and bruises all over his body. His hair had been shaved and the true nature of his injuries was there for all to see. He had a massive gash across the top of his head. The band members were all in shock and broke down; it was a terrible time for them all. Noddy stated

Post-recovery Don back on the road with Noddy.

flatly, 'Three days earlier we'd been doing Earls Court. We were on top of the world... None of that mattered any more... all that tour and everything meant bugger all really.' Jim Lea said, 'Y'know the guy looked like he'd been crucified. He's smashed up and his hair cut off; he's got a loin cloth and he's plugged into these machines.' Noddy concluded, 'At that point they said he won't last a day.' Don's family and friends were desperate; it looked as if he wasn't going to make it.

All the hit records and sold-out shows suddenly meant nothing when they realised they might well lose their dear friend. 'It was one heck of a shock,' says Dave. Noddy confirms, 'We really didn't know what was going to happen.'

Don describes how he came to after the accident: 'I do remember waking. I was shivering; I couldn't understand why. I was on a bed of ice

to keep my temperature down and I remember panicking, and pulling all the tubes out and trying to get out of bed.' He goes on to tell the story of what happened immediately after the crash itself: 'My life was saved by two nurses who happened to be going on duty just after the accident... they kept me alive 'til the ambulance came out. I've never yet been able to find out who those two nurses are – they'll never tell me.'

Don received sack loads of get-well cards from fans and other musicians in the music business. Slade were spectacularly popular, and everyone rallied round for their favourite bunch of 'yob rockers'. The cards and messages of support boosted the drummer's moral and made him even more determined to recover.

Because of his physical strength and will to live it was soon obvious that Don was going to pull through. Although it would take time, he was going to make it. It was incredible, and in no small part due to his physical fitness maintained by years of playing drums in a rock'n'roll band. Don had been an athlete in his younger days, and this also stood him in good stead. Family, friends and band alike were relieved he was going to survive. It was the best news ever, far greater than any hit record or No. 1 album.

Noddy says, 'Within six weeks he [Don] was back in the studio making a record with us. He had great determination. We had to go into the studio and start recording with him because the doctor said, "the sooner you can get him playing again, the better." It was only his own force and strength of willpower that brought him out of it.'

Don's tragic accident helped to re-ground the band and put things back into perspective. But there was one problem: the band had some shows booked and, with no drummer, they didn't know what to do. Jim recalls, 'We had a meeting at my house with Chas to decide what we were going to do. We decided to carry on.' Jim Lea's younger brother Frank was a talented drummer, and he was at Jim's house when the band had their meeting. Jim says, 'Frank was plumbing in the dishwasher and overheard the conversation. He said, "James, I'm your man!" As Frank says, 'The accident was terrible; it was extremely upsetting, tragic, but as I say, life carries on.'

The band agreed that Frank could take Don's place while he recuperated. A local newspaper ran the story with the headline, "From Plumber To Drummer!" Dave says, 'I remember doing one gig with Frank… he was a good lad, but he hadn't got Don's power.'

As soon as Don was better, all he could think about was playing drums. Within two months he was back behind the kit, and the band was almost back to full strength. They were relieved; they hadn't feel they could continue without Don behind the drums. Noddy says, 'It would certainly never have been the same; the magic was always the four of us together.'

Don's was a miraculous recovery that shocked everyone, including the doctors. Due to the accident he lost his sense of taste and smell, and suffered terrible amnesia and short-term memory loss. He couldn't remember conversations he'd just had or what time he was supposed to be at meetings. Even

worse was the fact that he couldn't remember songs. He would be OK once the band started and his memory had been jogged, but until one of the band had reminded him, he was a complete blank. 'We came to rehearse,' he remembers. 'I said, "Let's try 'C'mon Feel The Noize' – How's it go?"'…

But the band took it all in their stride, just glad to have their dear friend back. 'The memory thing was a problem with Don, but we just took it on board – it was the way it was!' says Jim Lea. Don admits, 'When I first realised I'd got amnesia, I used to fight like crazy, and that's the worst thing I could do.'

When it was time to do gigs, Don still had problems, even though his memory was slowly improving. Noddy recalls, 'So while I'm talking and chatting to the audience, Jim's behind me saying to Don, "It starts like this, that's how it goes," and by the time we come to start he was away – he could do it then.'

Sladest

In August 1973 the album *Sladest* was released while Don was still in hospital. It served as a stop-gap while he recuperated, and featured past hit singles, B-sides and favourite tracks.

Sladest was originally compiled for the American market, as many of the band's earlier triumphs had been missed over there. This album put a lot of the group's best songs, previously overlooked in the States, into one place, helping to improve the band's standing a little more Stateside.

Upon its release in Britain it immediately went to No. 1. Michael Gray wrote in *Let It Rock* magazine, 'Hundreds of thousands of people still dance, still like thundering, distorted music to batter into their skulls, and still accept nothing less from a Saturday night than the opportunity to go berserk.' Charles Shaar Murray calle *Sladest* 'an excellent album.'

The group's older songs from *Play It Loud* sat quite comfortably alongside more recent tracks. The reflective 'Pouk Hill,' the story of their photoshoot, has a morose candour that offsets the chipper 'One Way Hotel'. Noddy describes the song's inspiration:

'There were four of us, plus two roadies, in one hotel room. Six beds! It was pouring with rain and we were skint, not even the price of a pint between us. So we wrote this to pass the time.' Oh, how things had changed! They also included the early singles, 'Know Who You Are' and 'Get Down And Get With It', and there's no sense of disparity.

To keep the American fans happy, many of whom had never heard the earlier material, the album was rammed with hits, but really Slade could do no wrong. Noddy said, 'The time is right for us; the mass audience want it. We'd always done the same act, but the audiences didn't want it before. They just wanted to be cool and sit down and dig the music, and read deep things into it. But finally everybody got sick of that.'

The writing partnership of Holder and Lea had proved to be a runaway success. The only other pop writers of the period who could rival the pair were Nicky Chinn and Mike Chapman. Chinn and Chapman kept artistic control over the group Sweet. Sweet wanted to write their own material, but Chinn and Chapman only let them write their b-sides. Original producer Phil Wainman was eventually removed from the producer's chair by the songwriting duo who wanted more control of Swete's career. Chinn and Chapman wrote and porduced hits for other bands such as Suzi Quatro, Mud and Smokey. Nicky Chinn is quoted admitting, 'Michael and I were always autocratic with our bands. For a long time Sweet recorded only what Chinn and CHapman wrote with no chance of argument.

The two watched Slade carefully and always checked out their new releases. They knew that out of all the writers of the moment Holder and Lea were their biggest rivals, and there was much to be learned from listening to a Slade record.

The single 'My Friend Stan' was written while Don was in hospital, and released in September 1973. It went to No. 2, a healthier showing than the band had expected. Once again, 'Stan' found them in familiar musical territory: rowdy pop with a rock edge. Slade was beginning to feel that maybe it was time to try something a little different; not a major change of direction, more of a sideways move, with a view to something new. Slade had never had a political agenda or artistic pretensions; they just played rock'n'roll. Their musical philosophy was simple – have a good time! But there was a growing feeling among them, Chas Chandler included, that they wanted more.

Slade Bells

In 1973 glam rock had almost taken over, and the whole UK music scene was affected. Everything, it seemed, was glitter, stacked heels, flares, bright

The grand old Dame of Glam rock in all his pomp!

The smoothest Glam rockers on the
block. Roxy Music.

colours, feathers and make-up. This fashion wasn't just reserved for the regulars of glam – Sweet, Mud, Suzi Quatro, Gary Glitter and the Glitter Band and Wizard – even David Bowie and Elton John joined in with the trend inadvertently started by Marc Bolan and Slade. For a while, bands not usually associated with the glam scene adopted the fashion. Roxy Music wore glitter, make-up and sequins, as did lad rock band Mott The Hoople. Lead singer Ian Hunter said that when he was on *Top Of The Pops* in all his glam gear he felt like a 'Brickie in Gilt'. The whole UK music scene had gone glam, with Slade proving to be the most successful of them all.

The band's British record company Polydor always liked to release a Slade single in time for the Christmas market, and this year was to be no exception. The lads decided to record a special Christmas song, in the way that Fifties artists used to. Noddy and Jim had some ideas, and once they started, they realised they were

on to a winner. The music came in just one evening and was a mixture of some new ideas plus some old leftover bits the pair hadn't been able to find a home for. Noddy says, 'The basic melody to the chorus came from a song that was the very first song I'd written. The lyrics on it were really hippy, "So won't you buy me a rocking chair to watch the world go by, buy me a looking glass to look me in the eye..." Eventually Noddy went back to his parents' house and, with the aid of a bottle of whisky, he wrote the entire new lyric in one sitting. He simply made a list of everything he associated with Christmas. The song was called 'Merry Xmas Everybody'.

Slade's most enduring hit, and one of Britain's favourite Christmas songs ever, was actually recorded at The Record Plant in New York City in September 1973. Though Don Powell would later say that they recorded in the summer during a heat wave, it was in fact just a very hot autumn. John Lennon was in the studio next

One more run through 'that' single...

does at Christmas.' But though the song has made Jim Lea a lot of money and is almost like a pension to him and Noddy, he now hates it, bemoaning the fact that from almost November through til January you hear it everywhere. '"Merry Xmas Everybody" was written for Christmas Day,' he says. 'You don't start singing "Happy Birthday" to someone two months before the day.' He concludes, 'I wanted to write an anthem for Christmas Day but I never dreamt it would still be played 30 years later.'

Indeed, this song was to stay with them – and us – for many years to come. In the UK there really is no avoiding the song at Christmas time. Noel Gallagher, tunesmith for Manchester rockers Oasis, once asked jokingly, 'Doesn't it get re-released every year? I mean, that must have sold about 50 billion copies. Fantastic!' And Ozzy Osbourne quipped, 'Well, you always know it's Christmas in England, because [sings] "So here it is, merry Christmas..."'

'Merry Christmas Everybody' went straight in at No. 1, their third single that year to do so. It had 800,000 pre-orders, an immense pop achievement. Noddy believes that one possible reason for huge sales was the fact that when it was released, the UK was going through a terrible time. There were strikes, power cuts and a three-day working week. 'Merry Christmas' was the perfect antidote to all the depression that surrounded everyone, a tonic for a sick nation.

There was no stopping the boys from the Black Country. Neville, James, Donald and David literally seemed to own the pop charts, scoring hit after hit after hit. No one could touch them in the singles market. Years ago Chas Chandler had told them they could be 'the kings of the short pop song', and he was right. This was a perfectly-formed pop vignette.

The hit singles were coming thick and fast, but Slade's dream of becoming an albums band began to fade. Many of the Seventies groups would spend months in the studio recording an album and then maybe release one single from it; Led Zeppelin didn't release singles at all. Slade were victims of their own singles chart success. When they had a smash hit in the pop charts many rock fans would draw inexorably further and further away. Radio Luxembourg awarded them a trophy for 'bringing back glitter, energy, and excitement during the past

door recording his famous 'Mind Games' record, while Slade were rocking up a snow-capped Christmas hit in the unbearable heat of a New York fall. Even though it was September, the city was hot and sticky – hardly conducive to recording a Christmas song.

Noddy would always be proud of their perennial hit, stating: 'In that song are two of the best lines I ever came up with: "Does your granny always tell you that the old songs are the best? Then she's up and rock'n'rolling with the rest," which every granny year', but Dave Hill's costumes and the group's genuine bonhomie seemed to alienate many music fans, who preferred their music to be serious. Nonetheless the band were a phenomenon. There was no escaping Slade's ubiquity.

Old, New, Borrowed and Blue

Most bands would have a major problem on their hands having to followup such a massive hit as 'Merry Christmas Everybody,' but not Slade. The band recorded the album *Old, New, Borrowed And Blue* (released in the USA in 1974 as *Stomp Your Hands And Clap Your Feet* – apparently the Americans didn't understand the meaning of the UK title). It was released in February 1974 and went straight to No. 1. Slade simply moved on without missing a beat.

It was at this point that the band dropped using the misspelt titles, simply turning the 'N' around the opposite way instead. The gatefold sleeve sports all the Holder-Lea lyrics, and the cover features the lads with full Seventies hair-crime portraits. Musically, it's 12 tracks of pretty standard Slade fare, with only a few exceptions.

The opening track, 'Just Want A Little Bit' is the album's only cover, and makes for a moody start. It features Noddy at his screaming-at-the-top-of-his-voice best; a kind of 'Sweet meets Led Zeppelin'. 'When The Lights Are Out' is a harmless pop ditty that's almost Sixties in feel. Jim Lea features on lead vocal on this rather pedestrian shuffle. 'My Town' is a harder-edged attempt at some mean rocking featuring a classic Don Powell snare pattern; the bizarre 'Find Yourself A Rainbow' is 'barber shop quartet meets music hall' with a piano played by Tommy Burton. The lyrics for 'Miles Out To Sea' are the true story of a drunken night out enjoyed by all the lads. Jimmy's fluid bass lines mesh well with Don's sure-footed approach, but the track seems over-long. The final track on Side One, 'We're Really Gonna Raise The Roof' finds Noddy in full-on screamer mode while the band knock out some straightahead boogie rock with overtones of Status Quo.

Side Two opens with the boogie-woogie riffing of 'Do We Still Do It?' in which Noddy bellows, 'Come On, Come On, Come On' to great effect. 'How Can It Be?' asks 'How can a daydream change to a has-been?', a question the band will be able to answer in a few short years. Sparse arrangement and inspired melody makes this one of the highlights of the record. The upbeat single 'My Friend Stan' follows the Beatles-eque 'Don't Blame Me', while the thoughtful introduction of 'Everyday' leads into a forlorn Noddy giving a surprisingly tasteful vocal and Dave providing a reserved and melodic guitar solo. This is definitely one of the album's finest moments, and one of Slade's all-time greats – a perfect rock ballad before the genre really existed. The record closes with 'Good Time Gals', which boasts the swaggering feel of 'Free' and chord changes to boot. The suggestive, 'I wanted to touch your dream machine, in there anything goes...' lyric leaves you in no doubt as to what they're singing about.

All in all, *Old, New, Borrowed And Blue* is pretty standard stuff from the yobbos with guitars but 'Everyday' stands head and shoulders above all the other material. Overall the album lacks flair, and finds the band in a business-as-usual mood.

The album was released in America and the band continued to tour the States, where the situation had begun to turn around for them. Although they still hadn't achieved a major US hit, magazine articles and their concert reputation, grown largely through word of mouth, had improved matters tremendously. Dave Hill told journalist Michael Gross of *Circus Raves*, 'Now we're starting to sell out everywhere and we're topping the bill, too. It's a matter of covering areas. When they see us play, they like us, even if they haven't heard the records. Wherever we've played, we have a following.' On previous tours of America he commented, 'We were always getting slagged here; the reviewers just loved to put us down – it seemed a trend to give Slade a slagging. We just stopped looking, especially at the daily papers.' Dave told Gross of a local review the band had received. 'It was amazing. They got thousands of letters saying things like, "Hey man, were you there? Were your ears stuffed with cotton or something?" and the next week he wrote about Slade again and did a great review of our new single.'

The mirrored hat, the Yob guitar and outfit, the stripes and the checked gear. Yeah, Slade are all ready to go!

But there were still no hit records. 'Merry Christmas Everybody' was huge in Britain, but it wasn't even released in America. Undoubtedly, though, things were improving. Hill continued, 'I asked one kid how he'd heard about us. He said he'd tried to buy our records but the stores never had them – the radio never played our singles. But he'd heard about us in magazines. Somewhere in the mid-West – Toledo, I think – a kid showed up with his face painted all silver. They're wearing the clothes now and getting into the whole thing. It must be right. In Detroit we never had a great reception but the last gig was tremendous. The average age of the kids is about 16.' He added somewhat surprisingly, 'There was nothing worse than that "glam rock" tag;

it just isn't us! The new generation wants a good time. Our music is genuine. There's no hype cos we've been doing it for years! I get sick of labelling.'

The track 'Everyday' was taken from their latest album *Old, New, Borrowed And Blue* and released as a single in the UK. For Slade this beautiful ballad was a major musical departure musically and showed them in a new, more sensitive light. Noddy's voice worked extremely well in a more subdued style. The huge sing-a-long chorus was irresistible, and the song went to No. 2 in the chart. While the band had been concerned that their fans wouldn't accept this new direction, there was no need to worry. The single was a success and proved to band and audience alike that Slade could break away from their well-worn formula and still have hits.

SLADE IN FLAME

9

'The best rock movie of all time.'

Q Magazine

'Everybody wants to be in a movie, don't they?' said Noddy. 'But we weren't actually sure that we could pull it off.' In later years, he explained the genesis of the movie that was to become an enduring classic: 'Up until 1973 we'd been on the crest of a wave; first three years of the Seventies we'd lots of hit records and lots of No. 1 records – we'd had six No. 1 records. And our manager, Chas Chandler, he always took The Beatles as the blueprint of our career; he always wanted us to emulate or try to emulate the stages that The Beatles had gone through. We'd had all the No. 1 records, we'd gone straight in at No. 1 the first day of release with three records, and he saw it that the next career move for us would be a movie. We weren't actually that sure about it... None of us had ever acted before so it was a bit of a weird challenge for us, but he was sure we could pull it off.

'The next thing to do was to find a script or a story that he thought we could cope with. And we didn't particularly want to end up doing a slapstick, runaround type movie, speeded-up film and all that

Left: The shy, retiring Dave Hill.

because I thought that's what people would expect from us. Automatically they put Slade in that bag, which I thought was defeating the object of making a movie, 'cos several groups had done it before.'

The history of rock stars in movies goes back to the Fifties with Bill Haley and Cliff Richard, along with the King of rock'n'roll himself: Elvis Presley, who would eventually clock up an unprecedented 30-plus big screen appearances. In the early Sixties the idea of pop stars in film died off somewhat, until the beat boom began in the Sixties. The Beatles' manager, Brian Epstein, was keen to get his boys up there on the silver screen, and they would appear in five movies of their own, including *A Hard Day's Night, Help* and *The Magical Mystery Tour*. Although a feature, *The Magical Mystery Tour* was made for television and gave the previously untouchable Fab Four their first taste of bad press. The Beatles also wrote and performed the music in the feature-length cartoon *Yellow Submarine*, which featured them as cartoon characters with their voices dubbed by actors. Finally, there was the painful, almost unwatchable *Let It Be*, a study of a band falling apart.

Mick hits the silver screen in 'Performance'.

By the late Sixties even American manufactured band The Monkees had released their own film, *Head*, which oddly enough featured Frank Zappa, while The Rolling Stones' Mick Jagger appeared in *Performance* alongside Johnny Shannon, who played the part of a London gangster and would go on to appear in a similar role in *Flame*.

When the Seventies arrived the rock n' roll big screen flick was almost dead on its feet, until Ringo Starr decided to film 1970s pop star Marc Bolan on tour. *Born To Boogie* was the birth of the rockumentary; suddenly rock stars weren't required to learn dialogue, they could simply tour with a film crew following ten yards behind and immediately, they've got a movie.

Before the decade was over the floodgates had opened. glam rock spawned a number of such films, including Gary Glitter's regrettable 'Remember Me This Way', released in 1974. Gary's big screen appearance was a shambles; this particular flick had little or no plot, and wooden, self-conscious acting. Glitter himself was already overweight, which didn't help the movie either.

In 1975 *Never Too Young To Rock* was released, starring a series of lower end glam stars. Mud, The Rubettes, The Glitter Band (who had now achieved chart hits without Gary), Peter Noone, star of Herman's Hermits, and Slik, featuring Midge Ure, all appeared. While *Never Too Young To Rock* included a large number of hit songs, it had little to offer by way of a plot. It was a simple 'Carry On'-style romp, minus the cast, the script – and the laughs.

Rumour has it that Slade's fellow glam rockers Sweet were offered a movie only to turn it down because they felt that rock 'n' roll bands didn't make movies.

Godspell actor and pop star David Essex had a run of hit films in the 1970s. These were of a very high quality, raising the standard of the genre. The first was *That'll Be The Day*, a Sixties-based tale of the genesis of rock singer Jim, played by David Essex. Ringo Starr also appeared in the film in a supporting role, as did Keith Moon, the drummer from The Who.

The film's sequel, *Stardust*, finds our hero Jim finally becoming a huge rock star touring the world and slowly losing touch with reality, until eventually he dies of a heroin overdose in the final scene. So close to the bone was the latter film's story line that Ringo Starr, who was offered the chance to make a return appearance as the ex-fairground roadie Mike, actually turned the role down. Starr was replaced by '60's pop-star-turned-actor Adam Faith. Faith was well known for his role as the lead character in hit TV show, *Budgie*.

Ray Connolly of *Melody Maker* wrote the scripts for both *That'll Be The Day* and *Stardust*. In both films the supporting cast was made up of credible actors such as Robert Lindsey, Billy Fury, Rosemary Leach, Karl Howman, and Larry 'JR' Hagman. This influenced Slade, who would choose a strong supporting cast for their own movie.

In 1974 Dave Hill was considered for the part of Rocky in Richard O'Brien's classic cult movie *The Rocky Horror Picture Show*. This was because, as O'Brien points out, "glam was so big at the time." The movie was shot in 1974, slap-bang in the middle of glam mania, and when you listen to the *Rocky Horror* soundtrack you can tell. 20th Century Fox wanted Richard to flesh out the original stage cast (Tim Curry, Meatloaf, Nell Campbell and O'Brien himself) with glam stars to capitalise on glam's massive audience, so another star of the day, Gary Glitter, was also considered. O'Brien observed, "it made huge sense from their point of view. Big movie companies always think box office, first, last and in between". Eventually Richard convinced the movie studio to keep the original stage cast. The pop stars were never contacted and the movie went on to experience huge success.

More rock films would appear later in the 1970s and 1980s as the line between movies and music

Tim Curry camps it up as the 'Sweet Transvestite from Transylvania'.

Sid gets Vicious and does it 'his way' in
'The Great Rock 'n' Roll Swindle'.

blurred. The Who released Townshend's epic *Tommy*, the first rock opera, as a movie directed by the avant-garde Ken Russell in 1975. In 1976, fellow glam star David Bowie gave an impressive performance in Nic Roeg's sci-fi thriller, *The Man Who Fell To Earth*. It was hardly a rock 'n' roll movie, but David Bowie brought much of his rock star persona to the role, not to mention taking a great deal of the Mr Newton character with him when the movie was over. In the same year Led Zeppelin put their concert movie, *The Song Remains The Same* on the big screen.

Even punk rockers The Sex Pistols would make their own movie in 1980, *The Great Rock 'n' Roll Swindle*. Sex Pistols manager Malcolm McLaren was so impressed by *Flame* that he actually stole lines from it for *Swindle*. McLaren also happily admits that he cast Johnny Shannon, who played the sleazy band manager role in *Flame*, as the head of A&M Records in *Swindle*. Pink Floyd made their double album *The Wall* into a full-length feature in 1982. *The Wall* saw The Boomtown Rats' frontman and

future Knight of the Realm Bob Geldof make his big screen debut.

David Essex's two movies *That'll Be The Day* and *Stardust* influenced Chas Chandler and Slade to make their own film. They all felt that the band's success was sufficient to warrant making a movie – and if David Essex could do it, why shouldn't Slade? The band were a pop phenomenon and the most logical move seemed to be to expand into the movies. '(David) Essex had done *That'll Be The Day*. It was a natural step for Slade to make a film,' says Dave Hill. However, where *That'll Be The Day* and *Stardust* had almost been a glorification of the rock star, despite Slade's film would be nothing of the sort. They were determined to make a hard-hitting drama that revealed the music business's seedy underbelly.

The band wanted to not only appear in the film but act in it as well. This was a huge leap. They had never acted before; they were musicians and it would take a huge effort to pull the whole thing off. Noddy revealed his reservations, "None of us had ever acted

before, so we were dipping our toes into uncharted waters, definitely."

Chas Chandler touted for scripts. One of the movie ideas offered to the band was a comedy spoof of the 1960's horror movie *The Quatermass Experiment*, entitled *The Quite A Mess Experiment*. Noddy explains, "I was going to be Professor Quatermass, and Dave was going to be killed in the first fifteen minutes by a triffid, so that had to go out the window because Dave wasn't standing for that."

Andrew Birkin wrote the script that eventually became *Flame*. The band liked the story but felt it needed some changes, so Birkin and Richard Loncrane, making his directing debut, were invited out on the road with the band. Noddy said, 'When we read it we liked the story, or the basic idea of the story, but it wasn't true to life of what a band is all about. Unless you'd been in a band they tend to write about the myth of rock n' roll, and we wanted to show what rock n' roll was really like behind the scenes, not what the fantasy out front is, 'cos everybody sees all the glitz and glamour, and the parties and all that. But we wanted to show the other side of the business... we decided to take them on a tour of America, the two of them, to show them the reality of what life was like on the road, and whilst travelling... we would talk to them about our career, tell them stories about other band's careers, and that would be assimilated into *Flame*... We certainly didn't want to do a *Hard Day's Night*, we wanted a bona fide rock band story. The truth!'

Birkin and Loncrane only managed to last for about two weeks. Life on the road proved too much for them and they returned home, but they came back armed with stories and a new awareness of what it was actually like to be in a band.

The script they eventually produced wasn't a tale of Slade's rise to fame or some sugar-coated flick that made the music business seem fun and the band look pretty. The plot was a mixture of Slade's own experiences and tales of other groups' too. To

Ringo Starr as 'Mike' in 'That'll Be the Day'.

this, the writers added events they had witnessed themselves on their time with the band. Noddy reveals, 'We told them stories about loads of bands we knew, even the pirate radio station getting fired on with machine guns... all those stories are true... but not necessarily about Slade.' For instance, the scene where Noddy gets locked inside the coffin on stage actually happened to eccentric British rocker Screaming Lord Sutch. The final script was exactly what the band and manager wanted, more a gritty drama than a rock 'n' roll movie.

Slade transformed in 'Flame'.

The next challenge was deciding on a cast that would bring the realism of the film that Slade and Chandler desired. Alan Lake, the husband of British movie actress Diana Dors, was given a substantial role as the washed-up, past-it lead singer who Noddy replaces. On the first day of filming he had a drunken altercation on set and Diana had to beg for him not to be sacked. She had to chaperone him for the rest of the six-week shoot to make sure this didn't happen again. This set a pattern for later years when directors would hire Dors as Lake's chaperone, just to bring movies in on budget. The band found him enormously entertaining and liked having him

Dave as 'Barry' in 'Flame'.

around. Tom Conti played manager Robert Seymour, in his very first film role, DJ Tommy Vance had a part, and actors from police drama *The Sweeney* filled the remaining roles.

All four members of the band gave impressive performances, delivering their lines with no self-consciousness whatsoever. Here were four lads playing out a fictional version of what was actually happening to them, and they handled it with a self-assured aplomb that impressed everyone. Noddy admits, "We actually didn't do a bad job in the acting department really." This was something of an understatement; the band did an excellent job, and the critics were begrudgingly complimentary.

The band's on-screen chemistry had a gritty authenticity to it that regular actors could never have achieved. The lads found they were naturals. Don delivered his lines as well as any seasoned thespian could have, and Noddy was his usual chipper self, all mouth and trousers but absolutely convincing. Dave continued with his smiley on-stage persona; 'I never read the whole script anyway, I'd only read my part, I didn't even know what it was about half the time,' he later said. But it was Jim who was the real revelation. He seemed the most natural of them all, his character's overflowing enthusiasm becoming a brooding sense of growing frustration.

Extremely violent in parts, it looked as though *Flame* was set to receive an X certificate, which would have meant no one under 18 years of age would have been able to see it. Slade's fan base had a high percentage of young teenagers so this would have been commercial suicide. There had to be some changes to get the film past the censors, so it was heavily editing. However, even with the edits, the movie was undeniably hard-hitting.

Flame was not what Slade fans wanted from their favourite good-time group; neither was it what the critics expected from a band they viewed as pretty much a joke. But these boys had been through the mill of the music industry and they wanted to tell the true story. With *Flame* they achieved their goal of revealing the dark side of the music business that had hitherto remained hidden. Drummer Don Powell recalls, 'I

remember at the premier people said, "have you done the right thing by exposing the down side of the music business?"' Of course they had, though it was a totally unexpected move from the Brummie popsters.

Noddy says, "The public was shocked! They expected a funny, happy-go-lucky slapstick running around type of film, what they got was a reality look at what goes on behind the scenes, but it's got humour... today it's even more relevant, it's the story of a band that formed naturally with one another and they were taken up by a big London manager who had no concept of music and marketed them like baked beans. It's about their fast demise, a fast rise and fast decline that's cvcn more relevant now than then... that's the market place today with 75 per cent of music... but the film itself – I was surprised how it has lasted. Always gets voted one of the best films ever shown."

Flame was a critical success. And in 2003, nearly thirty years after its original release, the film appeared on DVD; and it has stood the test of time. *The Independent on Sunday*, *The Times* and *Classic Rock* magazine all gave the film five stars, with the latter calling it 'one of the bleakest and best rock films yet made.' *Q* magazine also gave it the five-star treatment and declared *Flame* 'The best rock movie of all time', while *Uncut* called it 'A fascinating and at times incredible piece of work'. Strangely enough, despite all this, *Flame* has had no more than two television screenings in the last thirty years.

Noddy said after one recent screening at the National Film Theatre, 'I was quite shocked! I didn't remember the film being that heavy, especially seeing the demise of the band again... it's stood the test of time partly because of the music and partly because of the gritty atmosphere, the way it's shot was like *Saturday Night Sunday Morning*.' But not everyone in the band felt the same way. 'Dave Hill hated the film, absolutely hated it! He won't watch it at all,' says Noddy.

A book was published to coincide with *Flame*, based loosely on the film script that finished up on the big screen. But the book contained a lot more bad language than you'd expect from a book aimed at such a teenaged market. Some scenes – most notably the one where the character Jack Daniels is pulled from the van and beaten – are far more violent in the book. This was one of the scenes that was edited from the shocking first cut.

Slade In Flame: The Soundtrack

In November 1974 the band released *Slade In Flame*, a soundtrack album to accompany the film. The band recorded yet again at Olympic studios and Chas Chandler remained in the producer's chair. They appeared on the cover in luminous suits, and the record reached No. 6 on the UK album chart.

Slade In Flame contained ten Holder-Lea compositions and no covers, and it spawned two British chart hits, 'Far, Far Away' and the wonderful 'How Does It Feel?', which served as the signature tune for the movie. 'How Does It Feel?' begins with a poignant intro on piano from Jim that slowly builds to a strident crescendo. The song only reached No. 15 in the singles chart – a veritable flop in Slade world. But now, some 30 years later, it sounds magnificent.

At the time not everyone was enthusiastic about the album. In *Let It Rock* magazine Simon Frith wrote, 'Slade's lyrics are strangely soft-centered, an easy trip into dumb philosophy and profundity – check out "How Does It Feel?"... The lyrical sogginess is a reflection of Slade's real problem: their lack of musical development. At stomping they can't better themselves, and Holder/Lea have immense melodic abilities even for ballads; they are masters of the catchy chorus. But these are three-minute skills.

'Listen through an album and the formulae begin to show. Slade albums grow on you 'til you notice the nasty things, like the essence of the Slade sound is the super-confident, super-speedy bass playing, but the lead guitar is lacklustre, elementary, and the drumming, good stomping stuff to dance to, is bad stomping stuff for listening. Britain's top Sixties groups – the Beatles, Stones, The Who – had sounds, songs and an extraordinarily high standard of technical, musician-like skills. Slade have got a sound and a potentially fine song-writing partnership, but their musical skills I'm not sure about and there lies their future.'

Unfortunately there was a hard truth to this stark observation. It was true that Slade's ambition to become an albums band had faltered. Instead they were seen as a good-time pop band who could write hit singles, one after the other. They could also rock like nobody's business, there was no denying that; but they just weren't accorded the same artistic respect as The Who, the Rolling Stones or Led Zeppelin.

Slade rock the masses. One of the hardest
working bands in rock 'n' roll.

Frith continued, 'Slade have reached the career time when the traumas start – break a successful formula or not? They must, to save them and us from boredom. But few groups survive such changes, and later the original style becomes the vision of the golden past – why did we fiddle with it? All Slade can do is the thoughtful. I think they can grow and prosper, but only if they begin to challenge themselves as musicians, go back to learning and worrying about their skills. Their next new venture (in between churning out the hits, guaranteed for a year or two more) should be an album with a new producer. Chas Chandler has exploited to the limits what Slade have got; they need someone to demand things from them they didn't know they had.'

LET'S STAY FAR, FAR AWAY

'They should have been the biggest thing since The Beatles in America.'

Ozzy Osbourne

Now every new band was trying to be a part of the glam scene. Bands such as Hello, Kenny, Sailor and Jet were all in on the act. There were also solo artists such as Alvin Stardust, who had previously released records under the name Shane Fenton, and Leo Sayer, who dressed up as a clown. Fifties show band Showaddywaddy, who had won TV talent show *New Faces*, were now classed as a glam band, as were little-known groups such as Fancy, Pandora and Milk 'N Cookies. Although some good artists emerged, such as Cockney Rebel and Sparks, they were pretty thin on the ground. At one point Queen were regarded as a glam band, as were 10cc and, most bizarrely, The Sensational Alex Harvey Band. Alice Cooper, the American shock-rocker, was seen as glam, though the US band who most deserved the tag were Kiss.

Left: Slade sample breakfast USA style.

After their movie-making experience Slade still felt unfulfilled, as though their career couldn't really go any further in the UK. Their ambition to be an albums band had pretty much failed; they couldn't compete with the likes of The Who and Zeppelin. But when it came to the singles chart, they ruled. Dave Hill observed, 'Although you're No. 1 in the charts, you still could be considered as a pop group; you're not being taken serious, like you're not The Who, the Stones or The Beatles.'

The band decided they wanted to concentrate on the American market. For years major success in the States had eluded them. Music journalist Ken Barnes wrote, 'The group may be picking up followers by way of increasingly enthusiastic concert reactions, but the recorded breakthrough for Britain's biggest phenomenon of the Seventies is still crucial, and continues to be shamefully long overdue.' They decided that now was the time for them to give the US their full attention. Britain was sewn up and

Left: Success on a level most other bands could only ever dream about.
Right: Adam Faith's prodigy Leo Sayer.

would always be there for them – wouldn't it? They decided to reverse the way they had worked before, basing themselves in America and travelling back to the UK and Europe for quick spats of promotion. The United States was their priority: it was 1975 and Slade were going to break America.

The band based themselves in New York and began recording at The Record Plant. They toured constantly and released their *Nobody's Fool* album in March 1976, featuring 11 original Holder-Lea compositions with no covers. It included a brass section and female backing vocalists, augmented the band that had obviously soaked up some US influences. A bluesy rock'n'roll workout, it featured some tasty down-and-dirty guitar licks as demonstrated in the laidback swagger of 'Do The Dirty'. The Beatles-esque 'In For A Penny' featured some solid, inspired guitar work from Dave, while 'Get On Up' sounded as though they'd written it especially for Kiss. 'LA Jinx' had funky flair mixed with the rolling bass lines and chord changes found on many of the band's classics. 'Did Ya Mama Never Tell Ya' had a catchy tune, but found the group attempting a Reggae groove. They were obviously trying to stretch themselves but they didn't quite pull it off, and *Nobody's Fool* reached a relatively low No. 14 in the UK album chart.

Although the rest of the album was a good-hearted attempt to entertain, it lacked punch and left many feeling a little cold. The band had lost its impetus; their laser-like direction and instinct for what to do next had let them down. They released the title track 'Nobody's Fool' as a single in the States, but it wasn't a hit. Don said, 'Concert-wise it [the USA] was great for us, we just couldn't get a record away!' Back in 1974 Ken Barnes had written in *Phonograph Record* wrote that for the USA, Slade were, 'Too pop for FM [radio] and too raucous for AM [radio].' This still held true. Other British artists, such as Elton John whose career had really taken off, had fared better out in the USA.

In the UK 'Let's Call It Quits' only reached No. 11.

For Slade this was a disaster. 'No. 11 in the charts can seem like the end of the road when you've had six No. 1's,' said Jim. Two more singles were released in the UK: the title track and 'In For A Penny', but they both flopped. This was a major shock to the band. It was inconceivable that they could release a single and not reach the top ten; it completely unnerved the band and left them feeling unsure of what to do next. Another album was recorded while they were still in America, but it remained in the can until they returned to the UK.

Slade's time in the USA had had cost them a lot, not only in terms of their career but also financially. As Jim Lea reveals, ' We all lost a lot of money.' As far as their career went, 'We'd blown it!' he said. Graham Swinnerton, a friend of the band and roadie of many years' standing, told one film crew, 'America was not ready and did not want Slade… America was coming

Another day another dollar, and some pinball, too!

out of Watergate, Vietnam. All it wanted to do was feel sorry for itself; it was not looking for a good-time band.' Unfortunately the infectious formula that had worked so well in the UK just didn't translate. As far as Slade were concerned, the USA remained unconquered. The band came home having grown tired of their lack of success Stateside to try and save their flagging career in Britain.

Slayed by Punk

Mid-1977 the band flew back to Britain. While they had been away punk had completely blown the music business apart in the UK. Although it hadn't taken over the radio it was all the music press wrote about, and all the old-school rockers were being ousted and denounced by the young punks. Teenage kids had a whole new set of heroes.

When Slade arrived they found a very different musical landscape to the one they left in 1975. Noddy told Jim Evans of *Record Mirror* why the band had briefly relocated to America: 'We were becoming a parody of ourselves and felt we needed to get away to revitalise. When we came back the music scene had changed a lot.' He would later concede, 'The late Seventies was strange for us – yeah, we were considered boring old farts, I suppose.' In fact the band were a major influence on many of the punks, who had grown up listening to Slade on the radio and watching them on TV, but in this nihilistic atmosphere no one could admit to liking Slade.

Dave Hill observed, 'It was black clothes, belts and studs, and chains coming off their noses, bad teeth, all sorts of stuff.' Jim called it 'year zero.' Noddy would later describe the movement as 'The revitalisation of rock music' but at this point it looked like the death of the band. However, as Sweet's singer Brian Connolly remembered, '"Punk swept away glam" was the statement the press made, but only the groups who were crying out

Promoting 'Nobody's Fools' on TV.

to be destroyed – so sure, The Rubettes, Chickory Tip, Lieutenant Pigeon, all that rubbish vanished without trace. But I remember one night being sat in a London club with Noddy or Jim, one of the boys, and in walks Steve and Paul from The Sex Pistols, and they only stopped short at kissing our feet. They bought the plonk, the lot, couldn't believe they'd met us!' And years later Steve Jones of The Sex Pistols would say, 'Slade never compromised; we always had the feeling that they were on our side. I don't know, but I think we were right.'

There is an argument that Slade were punks themselves, just without the sneer. The music wasn't that radically different but it was a different epoch, and things were changing. The depression that Slade had helped to lift in the Christmas of 1973 remained and now punk kids were expressing their frustration. There's no doubt that many of them were, two years earlier, all buying Slade records. Joey Ramone of the infamous New York

punk band The Ramones admitted, 'I spent most of the early Seventies listening to *Slade Alive*, thinking to myself, wow, this is what I want to do – I want to make that kind of intensity for myself! A couple of years later I found myself at CBGB's doing my best Noddy Holder.' And Noddy told journalist John Robb, 'I liked punk – there were some great bands in there; The Stranglers were fantastic. But it made it very difficult for us when we came back from the States.'

But it wasn't punk that damaged Slade; it was indifference. Sadly, their time had come and gone. By its very nature, pop stardom is always finite. The band had been so big, so successful; people wanted something new, something different. Much of the audience had simply moved on, and despite Dave Hill's best efforts in wearing punk designer Vivienne Westwood's clothes, most notably her 'Only Anarchists Are Pretty' shirt, Slade were out of fashion.

*Above: The earlier reluctant skinhead Dave shaves his head
whilst the boys go for that pirate, gypsy look.*

Left: A post-punk Noddy giving it everything in leather.

Whatever Happened To Slade?

The legend 'Whatever Happened to Slade' was an enigmatic piece of graffiti that appeared overnight in massive letters on a bridge over the River Thames. The band immediately adopted it for their next album, releasing *Whatever Happened To Slade* on Chas Chandler's Barn record label in March 1977, exactly a year after *Nobody's Fool*. Rocky and hard-hitting, it was a return to their original sound. Everything was stripped back to basics.

Listening to it now, it recalls Led Zeppelin and Bad Company. There are also shadows of Thin Lizzy's harmony guitars and Noddy sounds a little like gravel-voiced Roger Chapman of The Streetwalkers. *Whatever Happened To Slade* has some solid songs; it's rough-and-ready, if a somewhat stodgy mixture.

The album is pure Seventies rock, the very thing punk was challenging. In the Eighties all the 'glam metal' outfits coming out of America would sound like this, but for Slade it was a case of wrong place, wrong time. There is a definite sense of a 'hit hangover' here with the band unsure of exactly where they should be heading musically.

Although Slade still sold out big venues, they suddenly couldn't get any airplay. Radio refused to play their new material, and this hit them hard. Earlier in the decade they had been one of the biggest bands in the world, and now they couldn't get any airplay. In the press punk was marginalising Slade, but punk

didn't get played much on the radio. It was as though everyone had simply grown a little tired of the Slade sound. The band went back to a more 'rock' image wearing leather and denim, but Dave Hill went even further and shaved off all of his hair. This left him looking striking, if somewhat bizarre – but that was nothing new.

The Story Of Slade

In 1977 *The Story of Slade*, a collection of old songs, was released again on Barn records. The band continued to work on the live circuit but the standard of gigs deteriorated slowly but inexorably. Although their dedicated following never left them, eventually Slade began to perform their full-on rock show in cabaret venues.

Despite this fall from grace they still believed in themselves and still wanted more hits. In their hearts they truly believed they could achieve this, even though almost everyone else in Britain had just about written them off. Noddy wrote in his autobiography, 'I didn't find it depressing. I was still playing, still writing, still getting new ideas. None of us was enamoured with our situation, but at least while we were on stage, we enjoyed ourselves.'

Slade Alive 2

The band released *Slade Alive 2* in November 1978, again on Barn records. For them Europe was a constant source of income and they continued to play there regularly, finding enormous success in Poland, of all places. The revenue raised by these shows maintained the group's financial solvency. They would go wherever they could earn money

The band continued to work among the ruins

Left: Jim plays it cool.
Right: Slade on the TV show 'Supersonic'.

of their career; they were a group and they stayed together, no matter what. But by 1979 they really were out in the wilderness and began to find it hard to survive financially. Jimmy and Noddy were so dedicated to the group that they helped to fund the band from their personal writing royalties. Times were hard, very hard indeed.

Return To Base

Slade released the album *Return To Base* in October 1979, but the whole album had a cheap feel to it. The cover, a very simple affair, looked like a throwaway idea, and the band seemed to be following musical trends rather than leading.

In an attempt to keep up with the times, the straightahead, rocking track 'Ginny, Ginny' was released as a single on yellow vinyl, but failed miserably. 'Wheels Ain't Comin' Down,' the first track on the album, told the true story of Noddy and Jim on a plane in the USA, when the pilot announced that there was a problem with the plane. Noddy sings, 'All of my long life has flashed before my eyes.' 'Sign Of The Times' was released as a single, but it didn't chart. The band still seemed to be trying to find their way. There's the usual mix of roaring choruses and power riffs, but as an album it's a little uninspired.

Many of the songs on *Return To Base,* such as 'Nuts, Bolts And Screws', 'Hold On To Your Hats' and the aforementioned 'Wheels Ain't Comin Down' would appear again on Slade's next record, *We'll Bring The House Down.* This was the last album that Chas Chandler produced for the band.

Slade's Smashes

In 1980 Polydor records released the greatest hits package *Slade's Smashes,* but at this point things did not look good for Slade. The band realised the situation was serious. 'Money was difficult and records were drying up, and I thought what's going to happen?' said Dave. Jim Lea would later tell a film crew, 'The group was on the verge of breaking up around that time, yes. Dave was going to start up a wedding car business – not one of his brightest ideas.' Dave still had his Rolls Royce with the number plate YOB 1. The plan was rent the car out for weddings with himself acting as chauffeur. He did not continue with the business.

Chas Chandler, the man who had helped mastermind their success, was at a complete loss as to what to do. In the end his only suggestion was for Noddy and Jim, the writing team, to break away from Don and Dave to start a new band. This was desperation on his part, and Noddy was having none of it.

The boys were none too pleased when they heard about Chandler's suggestion, and the heart really went out of the band. They stopped playing live, and recording was non-existent. Noddy was left with the unenviable task of telling the crew that their services were no longer required. As the group's manager Chas Chandler should have shouldered this responsibility Noddy commented, 'I was annoyed that it had been left to me to do the dirty work, but then it usually was.'

Dave Hill was seriously considering leaving the group. He remembers, 'So I told Chas, and then he rang me up a week later and said, "I've had an offer." It's funny how things happen.'

His guitar wasn't the only thing Dave gave the 'Yob' monicker to.

READING FESTIVAL: THE COMEBACK

'Slade! A band that would never bend over.'
Kurt Cobain, Nirvana

In the summer of 1980 Chas Chandler got a last-minute call for Slade to play the Reading Festival. Ozzy Osbourne's new band Blizzard Of Oz had pulled out of the gig at the last moment, and the promoters needed a band quick. Even though Slade hadn't played together for months Chandler thought it was a great idea, as did the rest of the band. Dave Hill, however, was dead against it. He said he wanted nothing more to do with Slade. 'He was having none of it, Dave,' says Noddy. 'He didn't wanna do it, he was adamant. He'd refused.'

The other members of the band accepted that Dave couldn't be talked round. But Chandler knew this was a huge opportunity for the group and he was determined to change his mind. Dave told a documentary film crew, 'Chas was on the phone again: "are you thinking about it, Davey?" I said, "Yeah, I'm thinking about it." I must admit something was twitching at me, and then he talked me into it.'

Left: Rocking up a storm on the 'comeback' trail.

With all four members in agreement and keen to do the festival the band prepared to play the show. Having not played together for months and with such a big gig ahead of them, most bands would have had a couple of days rehearsal at least and then maybe even a warm-up show to prepare for the big event. Not Slade. They rehearsed on the day before the show; that was all the preparation they needed.

The next day they walked on stage and performed in front of 70,000 people. They had walked through part of the audience with their guitars and didn't even have backstage passes. Slade didn't need them; all the security guys had at some time worked with the band. They were old pals and they just let the boys through.

BBC radio DJ Tommy Vance came to see them in their caravan, and was convinced they were going to do well. He said it had been a pretty dull day so far and the audience were ready to be entertained. But the band wasn't so confident. If truth be told, they had no idea how they were going to be received. But they did sense something in the air.

They're Back! Reading Festival

Noddy says, 'There was this buzz about the place that it was going to be right for us somehow to play that day.'

When they walked on stage the place went wild. Slade's music actually *meant* something to the audience, and they went down a storm. Their natural bonhomie and familiar, uplifting songs really engaged the audience, as Noddy Holder hit them with every crowd-pleasing trick in the book. He radiated confidence. Having played to many a hostile audience and won them over, this was the ultimate challenge for the irrepressible singer. He fought and won easily, proving that he and the boys hadn't mellowed with age.

The audience all sang 'Merry Christmas Everybody' even though it was the middle of summer. Jim Lea was overwhelmed. He commented, 'We walked on stage. In 45 minutes we went from a no-hope to a huge, y'know, we were back, big time. The crowd were shouting out "Merry Christmas". So here we are middle of summer, heavy metal concert, tens of thousands of people all singing "Merry Christmas" – crazy.'

In the press area even the journalists and photographers were singing along and enjoying themselves, something unheard of in those cynical times. When they finished Britt Ekland was waiting for the band in their caravan and an endless stream of well-wishers wanted to shake their hands and congratulate them. The gig was an unprecedented success. Dave Hill admits, 'That night I couldn't sleep thinking about what I'd just done… and I was going to leave!'

Everybody had thought that Slade were dead – just a bunch of has-beens with no future, a nostalgia band at best – but this momentous show proved everybody wrong. Slade were back. Over the next few weeks they were on the front cover of every major rock magazine and weekly. Music papers that hadn't run even the smallest feature on the band now had them on the front cover.

However, the relationship between the band and their manager had soured to such an extent that it was irreparable. Jim and his brother Frank

Lea had their own independent label, Cheapskate, with Chandler and there were numerous problems. The relationship strained further until there was no contact between them. Jim no longer wanted Chandler to produce Slade records and eventually the band decided they no longer wanted Chas Chandler

to represent them. It was left to Noddy to tell Chandler that he was sacked as manager of Slade.

When Noddy requested a meeting with him, Chandler assumed that the frontman was going to quit and go solo. He was more than shocked when Noddy gave him his marching orders. Chandler

was, in Noddy's words, a 'heavy dude'. But he took the bad news in good grace and even negotiated a recording deal for the group with RCA records on the back of Slade's renewed success to leave them in a healthy shape. There was no fight, no argument; just the realisation that the partnership had reached the end of the road. In later years the group would be managed by Colin Newman, who is also in business with Frank Lea, first via Receiver Records and later Secret Records.

We'll Bring The House Down

Despite the problems between Slade and Chas Chandler the band released the single and album, *We'll Bring The House Down* on the Lea-Chandler owned Cheapskate Records in March 1981. *We'll Bring The House Down* was a hit in both Britain and Europe. European music magazine *Pop Rocky* called it 'A sensational comeback... After consistent hits in the Seventies, Slade probably thought they had their chips and nobody cared about them in the Eighties! Lead singer Noddy Holder laughs: "That's all over and done with now, we are more in demand now than ever and constantly run from appointment to appointment."'

Slade's luck had changed. Their guts and determination to see through the tough times had paid dividends, and their star was once again in the ascendent.

Till Deaf Do Us Part

Till Deaf Do Us Part contains some great rabble-rousing riffs and an infectious good-time vibe that you just know will go down tremendously well live. Some of the tracks became concert stalwarts – 'Rock'n'Roll Preacher' and 'Lock Up Your Daughters,' which sounds more than a little like Whitesnake's 'Fool For Your Loving', both appeared regularly. 'A Night To Remember' has an AC/DC vibe to it and with its salacious, leering lyric 'It's Your

Right: Post-punk Slade. Dave is pure Kings Road cool.

Body Not Your Mind' it's a song Mötley Crüe would be proud of. There are elements of Thin Lizzy and Ritchie Blackmore, with Dave Hill again proving his skill as a guitar player. Ultimately this is 'lads' rock' as demonstrated by the lyrics in 'Let The Rock Roll Out Of Control'. Noddy sings, 'Leather army, going barmy, giving it some stick/Leather jackets, make a racket, laying it on thick.'

Deaf hit the charts in Britain and was an even bigger success in Europe. German rock magazine Bravo wrote of *Till Deaf Us Do Part*: 'All four band members thrash away as if being hunted by the Devil! Despite all this noise, Slade are not simply steam-hammer rock. The music is significantly more intelligent than we are nowadays used to by heavy metal bands. Especially "Rock'n'Roll Preacher."'

That year AC/DC headlined the Donnington Festival and suddenly Slade found that they had a new, more 'metal' orientated following – even though they were still the same good-time rock'n'roll band they had always been.

Slade On Stage

In December 1982 Slade released *Slade On Stage* on RCA. *Cosmopolitan* magazine wrote, 'For 17 years, this British rock group have made ear drums vibrate. Their live performances are hellishly loud and one hundred times more exciting than today's hard rock bands - great!' Recorded in Newcastle's City Hall it finds the band on top form. *On Stage* is a marvellous mix of old stuff and some new tunes of the day.

The atmosphere is electric, the audience on the brink of hysteria. The band sound hard and heavy and as good as ever. Dave Hill excels himself on the first track 'Rock'n'Roll Preacher,' where he sounds like Angus Young of AC/DC fame. 'Take Me Bak 'Ome' comes alive here and proves that this is where the songs work best. They do a stripped-

The Amazing Kamikaze Syndrome

down version of 'Everyday,' which is a special moment. Noddy encourages audience participation at every opportunity. The album is a tour de force, and well worth digging out.

The band's stagecraft was well earned and ingrained. They never lost their magic in the live arena, no matter how big or small the venue. Noddy claimed, 'We never threw away our tricks. We just updated them' – and those tricks still worked extremely well.

Jim Lea and John Punter produced the album, giving it an Eighties sound that made the group seem modern, though it wasn't what many fans expected from Slade.

Left: Back 'home' on 'Top of the Pops'.

However, this was the band's most successful record for years. In April 1984 it was released in the States with the title *Keep Your Hands Off My Power Supply*.

Run Run Away

Slade were well and truly back. 'Run Run Away' cemented their newly regained position as major rock players, especially in America. The band had now signed to music giants CBS records and the single found itself on heavy rotation on MTV. This resulted in the single rocketing into the Billboard chart, reaching No. 20.

A major contributing factor to their success in the US was the fact that 'poodle rockers' Quiet Riot had covered 'Cum On Feel The Noize' and gone top five with it in the States. Quiet Riot also had a subsequent hit with another Slade song, 'Mama Weer All Crazee Now'.

'Run Run Away' was their first ever top-20 hit single in the United States. Things were great once again in the Slade camp. Finally the band were experiencing some success in the USA. Noddy remarked, 'I suppose our time had come in America.'

The band was now 'self-managed', but in America, Slade took on the services of music manager-svengali Sharon Osbourne, the wife and manager of fellow Brummie, Ozzy Osbourne. Noddy and Ozzy were friends from way back and Noddy would go to parties thrown by Sharon's father Don Arden, who had been a manager since the 1950s. There was a lot of history between the two camps so the band agreed for Mrs Osbourne to look after their career in the US. She had pretty much performed miracles with Ozzy in the States, where he was now officially *huge*. This was a wise move on the band's part, because if anyone could capitalise on Slade's newfound success in America, Sharon could!

Unfortunately, it was over before it began. A six week tour supporting Ozzy was booked. The

Above: Mr Holder and Mr Hill: 'You write 'em, I'll sell 'em.'
Right: The Prince of Darkness in his Black Sabbath days.

band played a few warm-up shows and then joined Ozzy's tour, but after the first date Jim Lea was sick. He said, 'I began to feel very ill and I didn't know what it was – I felt as if I was dying.' Noddy remembers, 'We came off stage and Jim collapsed in the dressing room.' Jim had hepatitis; there was no way he could go on the road so Slade had to pull out. For them, the tour was over before it had even begun.

Once again it seemed as if the band were jinxed when it came to the US. Ozzy said, 'Every time they tried to do America, something would happen.' For a while Noddy based himself in LA to do as much promotion on the record as possible, but the momentum was lost, and in the music industry it's all about keeping things moving.

Noddy recalls that the band did a final promo show in Cleveland, Ohio. 'We were standing on the stage playing, don't forget Jim's ill as well. The tapes are going, I'm singing live, it's like doing a TV show in front of thousands of people – I mean it was like karaoke, if you like – and I'm thinking, what the hell are we doing? I got in the car and I said to the others, "This is never going to happen with this band again!'

1984 was to be the last time Slade played live together. Years later Jim Lea observed, 'It was just one of those points in history, just like The Beatles at Candlestick Park. We didn't know that was it.' He added, 'The end of us live was the end of the band, really.'

The band returned to Britain and another tour of the UK was planned. However, the recent schedule in the States had taken its toll on them and no one was that enthusiastic about going on the road again. And then something surprising

started to happen: their egos began to take over. Having been through it all ten years earlier they should have known better, but they had grown no wiser and the success, for which they had worked so hard and waited so long, began to tear them apart. Jim wanted to produce the band and Dave insisted the group record more of his songs. Cracks began to show.

Slade's Greats

In 1984, Polydor released yet another greatest hits package in an attempt to cash in on the resurgence in Slade's career.

Rogues Gallery

With Jim Lea finally recovered from hepatitis the band continued to record as they were still contracted to RCA. *Rogues Gallery* was produced by John Punter and released in March 1985. Heavy metal magazine *Kerrang* wrote, 'What we're presented with here is ten songs that are totally brilliant choruses; you just can't help but want to sing along with Noddy every time he wraps his sandpaper vocals around one. This band has always been about hooks and here they're dripping aplenty!'

'All Join Hands' was a Top Ten hit for the group in Britain, but the problems for the four Black Country boys slowly grew bigger and bigger. Things were not going well for any of them. Don Powell had developed a drink problem; Noddy split from his first wife Leandra with whom he had two daughters, Charisse and Jessica. The relationship had broken down due to Noddy's long periods of absence working away for months at a time with the band. In addition, Jim Lea was at a loss as to what direction the band should take next and guitarist Dave Hill frustration with the record company rejecting his songs continued to build.

Crackers: The Christmas Party Album

A bizarre collection of covers and Slade hits, *Crackers* was released on Telstar/Castle records in November 1985. This somewhat surprisingly reached No. 34 on the UK album chart and included the classic, 'Santa Claus Is Coming To Town'. 'The Okey Cokey' a medley of 'Auld Lang Syne' and 'You'll Never Walk Alone' also appear. Slade's original songs include old favourites 'Cum On Feel The Noize' and 'Get Down And Get With It', with more recent material such as 'My Oh My' and 'Run, Run Away'. Of course, 'Merry Christmas Everybody' just had to be included. *Crackers* was a low point for the band, who many fans felt shouldn't have agreed to make an album such as this.

You Boyz Make Big Noize

The album *You Boyz Make Big Noize* was released in April 1987 on RCA. Queen producer Roy Thomas Baker was brought in, but it was a disastrous choice. Baker used a slow, painstaking recording process that didn't fit Slade's good-time rock'n'roll vibe. They liked to work fast, and Baker's fastidious approach wasted valuable time and ate into their minimal budget. He finished just two songs. The band wasn't happy: the budget was all but gone and what Baker did deliver they felt just didn't measure up. They re-mixed his tracks and finished the album themselves. Even the record company, who had recommended Baker in the first place, had to admit that what he had delivered was way below par.

This album had a very modern sound; the band dabbled with sequencers and new recording techniques. Later listenings reveal *Boyz* to be a strong album, but at the time the band were exhausted and exasperated by Baker's slow production style. It was

A still from the 'My Oh My' promo video.

another major blow to the morale of the group and one they would never recover from.

Noddy had had enough and founding member Dave didn't want to tour any longer. Dave and Jim wanted to carry on and Noddy suggested they get another singer, but they were having none of it. How could you replace one of the greatest voices in rock'n'roll? It was all becoming too much like hard work for all of them. It looked as though things were finally falling apart.

to try something a little different for a while. Although he didn't want to split Slade – he just wanted to take a break – he realised that maybe it was time to move on.

It was an amicable split. They all stayed in contact and remained good friends. Noddy sang on one of Dave's records, a cover of the Everly Brothers' tune 'Crying In The Rain', and together Jim Lea and Noddy produced the album *Play Dirty* for the British all-girl group Girlschool in 1983.

Let's Call it Quits

There was no specific problem that led to Slade's split; no fanfare, big announcements or fuss. The band simply ran out of breath. It seemed that Slade were well and truly over.

Offers were coming in for Noddy to do acting work and diversify. He felt he owed it to himself

The Slade Collection 81–87

The *Slade Collection* was released in 1991 on RCA records and featured hits like 'Run Run Away', 'My Oh My' and 'Gudbye T' Jane'. This was an attempt on

RCA's behalf to get as much out of their Slade back catalogue as they possibly could.

Wall Of Hits

In December 1991 Polydor, who still handled the majority of the band's back catalogue, decided to release a big-budget greatest hits package for the Christmas market titled *Wall Of Hits*. They planned a full promotion including expensive TV advertising. The record company asked the band if they would be willing to record a couple of new songs to include on the record, a trend that had become prevalent with recent hits collections. They agreed and once again Slade reconvened and recorded two Jim Lea songs: 'Universe' and 'Radio Wall Of Sound'. They were both released as singles and backed by Dave Hill compositions. 'Radio Wall Of Sound' made a small dent in the UK charts, but the very un-Slade-like 'Universe' disappeared without trace.

This really was the end of the line for Slade and would prove to be the last recordings the band ever made together.

The Slade Collection 79–87

The Slade Collection Volume 2 was released in 1993 on RCA and was much the same as the previous collection of the band's recordings, but this time going back to 1979. This was a further attempt by RCA to capitalise on their Slade back catalogue.

Right: Glamming it up, like only he can... Mr Dave Hill.

WHATEVER HAPPENED TO SLADE NEXT?

'Whatever happened to bands that rocked like Slade? Y'know, that no-bullshit, fuck you, in your face, we're bad-as-hell-and-we-know-it kind of band?'

David Coverdale, Whitesnake

Slade 2

In 1992 Don Powell and Dave Hill announced they were going out to play shows under the name 'Slade

Left: Moving with the times, having hits in their third decade.

2'. Jim Lea was against it, saying it would taint the achievements of the original band. But ultimately, his objections came to nothing, and the fans were more than happy to see this new incarnation of the group. No one was terribly offended and the band's legendary status was not diminished in the slightest.

Greatest Hits: Feel The Noize

Polydor released yet another Greatest Hits package in 1997. Manchester rockers Oasis had covered Slade's 'Cum On Feel The Noize' in 1996, leading to renewed interest in the band. This hits package capitalised on the situation.

The Genesis Of Slade

Cherry Red Records released *The Genesis of Slade* in 1997. This was a compilation of rare, early recordings featuring various members of Slade. It includes tracks by The Vendors, Steve Brett and the Mavericks and The 'N Betweens.

Slade Again

The line-up of Slade 2 saw various members come and go. In 1998 the band dropped the '2' tag and reverted to Slade. Bass player Trevor Holliday left the group in the September of 2000. His replacement was bassist Dave Glover. Previously a member of Brian Connolly's version of Sweet, Glover would eventually be sacked from his position under bizarre circumstances.

In 2002 *The News of the World* reported that the original line-up was going to reform for five nights at London's Brixton Academy, and although this story came to nothing, the Academy was over-run with ticket requests.

Glover was asked to leave the band on 22 January 2003 over his alleged 'relationship' with Rosemary West, wife of mass murderer Fred West. The musician gave an official statement to the national press about his relationship with West on 24 January, saying, 'I

am not, and was not planning to marry Rosemary West. I wrote to Rosemary West first in March 2002 after reading of her decision not to proceed with her appeal in the European Court. I firmly believe that Rosemary West was wrongly convicted of murder, and I wrote to tell her that I was sorry that she felt unable to proceed. Since then we became good friends although press reports that we "spoke every day and exchanged hundreds of love letters" are completely untrue. I am no longer in contact with Rosemary West.' He remained sacked.

Get Yer Boots On/ The Best Of Slade

In 2004 another its package, *Get Yer Boots On* was released in the States amid rumours of a full-blown reunion from the original members. Again, the rumours came to nothing. Christmas 2005 saw the release of *The Best Of Slade*, a greatest hits CD accompanied by a DVD full of classic performances from the band at the height of their career.

Slade: the Current Line-Up

Steve Whalley, the man with the unenviable task of taking over Noddy Holder's position on vocals and guitar, had done a sterling job but left to pursue a solo career in June 2005. Singer and guitar player Mal McNulty (ex-member of guitar player Andy Scott's version of Sweet) has now taken over the front man responsibilities and continues to do a marvellous job.

The current line-up also features John Berry, an ex-member of Seventies glam band Les Grey's Mud on bass. He also has a regular cameo part on TV soap *EastEnders* selling the *Big Issue* magazine outside the tube station.

Slade 2. Steve Whalley fills some big shoes.

Suzi Quatro's ex-husband Len Tuckey now manages Don and Dave's Slade.

Noddy Holder

Since leaving the band Noddy Holder has forged an impressive career as an actor and broadcaster. His TV appearances include *The Grimleys*, as music teacher Mr Holder, Vic Reeves and Bob Mortimer's *Shooting Stars* TV quiz show, *Parkinson, Jonathan Ross, The Frank Skinner Show, The Paul O'Grady Show, Never Mind The Buzzcocks* and even *Bob The Builder*. In 2000 he played Stan Potter in the long-running soap *Coronation Street*, and he was also a bi-weekly presenter and reviewer on *The Mark Radcliffe Show* on BBC Radio 2. In 1996 he was caught by Michael Aspel on *This Is Your Life*.

Vic Reeves and Bob Mortimer also did a spoof of Slade as part of their comedy sketch show *The Smell Of Reeves And Mortimer*, featuring Vic as Noddy and Bob as guitarist Dave Hill. The band loved the send-up, Don calling it, 'Brilliant, absolutely brilliant!' Dave Hill approved, too: 'Oh, those Brummie accents!' 'Really, in a surreal kind of way, it's pretty much what we were like in them days!' Noddy concludes.

Noddy has appeared on many TV shows as a guest, an actor or sometimes providing a voice-over. Once more he has become a true household name. He now lives in Cheshire. He married his long-term girlfriend Suzan Price at a secret ceremony in Cheshire on 7 April 2004. They have a son together, Django. In 2000 he was awarded an MBE for services to music and his wacky TV ad campaign for the bar snack brand Nobby's Nuts, began on 1 May 2005, shows he's still not taking himself too seriously.

In 2002 Noddy told rock journalist and broadcaster John Robb, 'We were the biggest-selling singles band in the UK in the Seventies, and we never had any critical acclaim. We do get sort of pushed to the back of annals in pop history despite all the hits we had from 1971 to 1991. But the tide has turned with new young bands covering our songs, like Oasis with "C'mon Feel The Noize", so people look on us in a different light, not just as a cartoon pop act. We always got looked on with affection – as a happy-go-lucky, good-time fun band – and that is what we started out to be. We never had a heavy message in our music, just good pop rock songs. We were a great live band; we had a massive live following all over Europe before we ever had a hit in Britain. The hits were the icing on the cake.'

On September 6 2002 Jim ended almost 20 years of exile from the stage by playing a gig in aid of protesters fighting the Wolverhampton bypass. That same day he told *The Wolverhampton Express and Star*, 'I'm not into celebrity or high profile stuff; I've never stopped writing, I've got enough stuff to fill ten albums. Slade was the most amazing band, touring all over the world with these guys, I'm never going to replace that but it was fantastic.'

Don Powell

Don continues to play the drums in Slade 2, where he and Dave still enjoy a sizeable success playing to packed-out venues and they travelling as far afield as Russia. He currently resides in Denmark with his girlfriend Hanne, and has recorded a solo drum album, entitled Let There Be Drums. He still has the master tapes of the sessions and plans to get around to finishing it one day. Asked when he would consider giving up playing, he replies, 'I love playing the drums and as soon as I stop enjoying it, I will finish… but I have the best job in the world, I travel the world doing something that I love, and I get paid for it! I've been lucky, so lucky, and I'll always appreciate it.' Don has also written a children's book called *The Bible Brick*, which will have an accompanying CD of songs he has written.

Asked in a recent interview if there would be a reunion of the original band, Don replied, 'Well, they say never say never, but to be honest I can't see it. From the bottom of my heart, I can't see it happening.'

Jim Lea

A father of two, Jim Lea lives in Staffordshire. He invested in property and in the Nineties he spent a long time in London studying psychotherapy. Jim is prolific; he still writes and records, and has released records under many different guises: The Greenfields Of Tong, The Clout and Gang Of Angels. He currently records under the name Whild.

Dave Hill

Also living in Staffordshire, Dave Hill continues to play in Slade 2 with Don Powell. He is a Jehovah's Witness and has served on the parish council. In his spare time he teaches music at the local school.

The band are constantly asked if they are going to reform the original line-up, but it's something that seems less and less likely as the years roll by. As Noddy says, '"When are you going to get back together with Slade?" That's all I ever get, but y'know, it ain't gonna happen. I don't know why people can't accept that fact.'

As for Dave, 'I thought we might do something for the Millennium,' he said. 'I'm sure somebody would love us.' When asked about Noddy, he admitted, 'I wish he was still with me.'

Slade: A Monument to their Own Success.

It's been said that the boys from Slade were so ugly they could have been the missing link. Well, they are. They're the missing link between The Beatles and Oasis; the missing link between Small Faces and The Jam; between Thin Lizzy and Bon Jovi, Alice Cooper and Kiss, the Rolling Stones and Aerosmith, The New

York Dolls and Hanoi Rocks. Slade are the connection between glam and punk, pure pop and Eighties rock. To the list, add Lennon and McCartney, Jagger and Richard, and, of course, Holder and Lea.

There's no denying this working-class rock'n'roll band's domination of the early Seventies and their subsequent international influence. As Noddy told John Robb, 'A lot of bands over there [the USA] claim we were an influence.' Oasis's Noel Gallagher called Slade, 'Fundamentally more important to the development of music than Radiohead.' British music journalist Chris Charlesworth believes Slade would have been taken a lot more seriously had it not been for the way that they looked. He claims this happened to ABBA, but believes critics have now started to realise just how important they actually were – despite their dress sense. He believes that music critics will one day re-evaluate Slade in the same way. We, the authors, would like to think that this book is already part of that revaluation.

Should Slade ever did decide to get back together with the original members it would be a huge success; of that there is no doubt. If they made a new album it would probably go to No. 1, and many a dad would lecture his kids, 'This is how it should be done!' And if they toured, the shows would sell out in hours… Oh yes, we can dream, we can dream!

But as it stands we have Dave and Don's fine version of Slade on the live circuit and CDs of the band's many recordings. There's also a growing number of DVDs covering various aspects of the group's career to keep us entertained, Slade style. And every year around December we can all look forward to singing along with the boys once more. You know there's no escaping it: come on, all together now: 'So here it is, Merry Christmas, everybody's having fun… '

The virtuoso Mr Lea.

SONG-BY-SONG

GUIDE TO THE HITZ

Get Down And Get With It

From the get-go the lads made rowdy pop records, and this reached No. 16 in June 1971. Noddy's voice sounds absolutely amazing – it seems to tear a hole in the speakers. As well as playing bass guitar, Jimmy Lea adds a traditional rock'n'roll piano part to the proceedings, harking back to the Little Richard roots of the song. Dave Hill provides some tasty licks to the traditional 12-bar blues progression, and contributes a screeching guitar solo.

Produced by manager Chas Chandler, the final choruses are a frenzy of guitars, stomping feet and 'Yeah, Yeah, Yeahs' from Noddy. It's a great record, and of course their breakthrough track. Noddy said that after the release of 'Get Down': 'It just went ballistic.' Music journalist Charles Shaar Murray described the single as as 'a fine piece of rabble-rousing.'

Coz I Love You

Slade's very first No. 1 single reached the top in October 1971. Jim Lea remembers, 'This was the first time that we deliberately sat down to write a commercial song. We hadn't had to worry about follow-ups before – we hadn't had bloody hit singles. We wrote it in about half an hour. We just got the feel right early on; we seemed to have the right formula, simplicity and atmosphere.'

Left: The one and only Mr Neville Holder.

Jim's multi-instrumental talents were used wherever possible. Here, he adds an electric violin to great effect. The tune relies on straight fours played on guitar with a shuffle groove that shifts the proceedings along underneath. The echoed claps bring the track alive and give it a 'skip' feel while Noddy and Jim spar on the outro, swapping lines between voice and violin. The overall feel is controlled, but the groove makes it almost impossible not to tap your feet – and the tune is unforgettable.

Look Wot You Dun

Originally by Jim Lea and Don Powell, 'Look Wot You Dun' reached No. 4 in February 1972. The song had been lying around for years, but the band felt the chorus was weak. It was re-written by Holder and Lea and became a massive hit, but the initial idea came from the rhythm section. This is why it's one of the few songs credited to Holder, Lea and Powell.

It starts with an uncharacteristic piano introduction, which sets a subdued tone for the whole song. It works tremendously well, and is a direction the band would have done well to mine further. Don pounds the beat on heavy fours as the band rocks steadily back and forth in the groove before shifting gear into a 2/4 time signature and the track turns and bounces along metronomically. This was a musical trick Slade employed a great deal and one of the elements that gave the songs their trademark 'stomp' feel.

Take Me Bak 'Ome

This reached the top of the British charts in June 1972. The band tear through the song with a lethal ferocity. It's a real rockin' party anthem that features a classic riff played by Dave in his inimitable style and Don Powell's trademark snare drum beat. The huge claps dominate from the second verse and Noddy's voice rips your head off.

When asked about the similarity of many of the songs, Noddy replied, '"Look What You Dun" and "Take Me Bak 'Ome" were the only two on which I could hear any real similarity.'

'Take Me Bak 'Ome' has that joyous feel to it that many bands simply can't achieve. It's bursting with an energy and enthusiasm that really puts a smile on your face. When you listen to Slade it's hard to remain in a bad mood and this is a prime example of the band at their rockin', devil-may-care best.

Mama Weer All Crazee Now

In 1973 Ken Barnes, writing in *Rolling Stone* magazine, called 'Mama Weer All Crazee Now' 'the quintessential rocking anthem', and he was spot on. Charles Shaar Murray told *NME* readers, 'It's the ultimate *Clockwork Orange* violence-and-insanity-for-the-hell-of-it rock song because it's so totally un-self-conscious.'

'Mama' is a classic raucous rock'n'roll anthem that reached the heady heights of No. 1 in September 1972. All the classic ingredients appear; it's so honest and direct, it's irresistible.

Gudbuy T' Jane

A stomping classic that was huge in the UK, 'Gudbuy T' Jane' reached No. 2 in Britain but only slightly dented the lower region of the US chart. It was written with blithe nonchalance at the end of a recording session and still remains an all-time

favourite. The track opens with Don's stuttering, almost frenetic snare drum beat that relentlessly cuts a swathe through the entire song. Added to this is a Rolling Stones' flavoured maracas and shaker. Usually the band pound home the title of the song in the glorious choruses but here the title is used in the more subdued verses with the chant of 'I say you're so young' as the chorus hook. The 'All Right. All, Right, All, Right, All, Right,' section was lifted unaltered from Elvis Presley's mid-Sixties song 'Kissin' Cousins'.

Noddy explains the inspiration behind the song: 'It was during our American trip in September 1972. We were on this telly chat show in San Francisco and there was this chick who just sat beside the compere – that's all she did, just sat there, looking gorgeous. She had a pair of shoes, called them her "Forties trip boots". She thought they were marvellous, though you could buy them in any Oxford Street store over here. She lost them just before the show and we helped her turn the place over to find them.'

Cum On Feel The Noize

The song 'Cum On Feel The Noize' made history for Slade as it went straight into the British charts at No. 1. This was a tremendous achievement for the band, and one that would set a precedent for all future releases. Noddy reveals part of the reason for writing the song: 'We went to look at the hall after the gig. It was devastated. Everybody seemed to have gone crazy that night.'

In 1995 Slade fan and legendary record promoter Dylan White suggested to Noel Gallagher, while he was doing a guest spot as a DJ, that he should play some Slade. This led to Gallagher discovering 'C'mon Feel The Noize'. The guitar player immediately decided the song would be great for Oasis. He admitted, 'If it wasn't for [White], we wouldn't have done the Slade cover really.' He continued, '"C'mon feel the noize, girls grab the boys, we go wild, wild, wild..." it just sounded like an Oasis song, y'know?'

Holder and Lea, another TV gig.

Jim Lea confesses, 'It's a bit uncanny for me when I play people new stuff and they say, "Ah, this sounds like Oasis," and I think, isn't this like putting the cart before the horse?' Noddy put it into perspective when he said, 'I went to see Oasis when they did Maine Road, and they came on and did it as the encore. It was great seeing 40,000 kids singing along to it, a song that was 20 years old – more than 20 years old – and the audience were singing along to it in the Nineties.' Noel Gallagher said, 'I hope it was as good for him [Noddy] as it was for us.'

Quiet Riot and One Way System both covered 'Cum On Feel The Noize' in 1983.

Skweeze Me, Pleeze Me

This was the second song of Slade's 'straight-in at No. 1' hat trick. Going in at No. 1 in 1973 was a rare feat because you had to sell a huge number of records to get there. The next band to go straight in at No. 1 was The Jam with 'Going Underground' in 1980.

'Skweeze Me Pleeze Me' was written because it was felt the group needed a song that the audience could join in with instantly, even on the first listen. They achieved their goal with the song's massive 'Woah, woah' sections. 'Skweeze' is yet another party monster of a track and Noddy's vocal in the outro section is amazing. His ad-libs are inspired, and as the track fades, you just want to hear more.

My Friend Stan

The boys recorded this as a stop-gap track that was released after Don recovered from his car crash. They were most surprised when it reached No. 2 in the UK chart. It was kept off the top spot by the theme from TV show *Eye Level*. At this point the lads stopped misspelling their titles. Charles Shaar Murray wrote in the *NME* in September 1973, 'According

to the ads, Slade's next single is called "My Friend Stan". That's right, not "F-r-e-n-d" but "F-r-i-e-n-d." What's conventional spelling doing on a Slade record? They're not softening up, are they?'

Asked if the band would ever change their style, Noddy replied, 'We've found our format and we're sticking to it… When people say we're "mindless rock and roll" I like it, that's a nice description. We don't aim for the head anyway; we're a rock and guts band.' Here we find the boys sticking to their format successfully. "Mindless rock'n'roll" it may be, but boy does it work.

Merry Christmas Everybody

The perennial classic from which at Christmas there is absolutely no escape. Christmas isn't Christmas until you've heard this; there's hardly much chance of escaping it. Noel Gallagher from Oasis said that his favourite part of the song was when Noddy yells, 'It's Christmas!' at the end of the track. 'Pure emotion,' he observed.

Slade in their heyday-full-on-glam days.

'Merry Christmas Everybody' went to No. 1 in December 1973 and stayed there for a month, right over the Christmas period and into the next year. It was in the chart for a total of 25 weeks. What's more, it's been constantly on release since it was first released in 1973. It has never been deleted; you can always order a copy no matter what time of year it is.

'Merry Christmas Everybody' was recorded in New York in September 1973. The band attempted to lay down the track a few times but they were never happy with it. Eventually they stripped it back down to its basics and recorded the song one instrument at a time. This approach was standard practice for many bands, but not for Slade. It was the first time that they had ever attempted to record a song in such a fashion.

Everyday

This wonderful Beatles-esque ballad went to No. 3 in April 1974. 'Everyday' was a welcome departure from the 'have-a-good-time' vibe Slade were most famous for. Jim commented, '...it's the gentler side that we aren't remembered for... we're remembered as the guys who make a lot of noise, but we didn't always.' Almost a lament, the track has a lullaby quality to it. Noddy's voice works so well in this register and it's a shame the band didn't record more of these kinds of songs. The good time material worked so well, but 'Everyday' shows real brevity.

The Bangin' Man

'The Bangin' Man' reached No. 3 in July 1974. The band are in an upbeat, party mood, and 'Bangin'' finds them in familiar territory. Noddy's voice in the last verse is pushed to its absolute limits, leaving him sounding almost super-human. Just how did he sing like that?

Bon Jovi would later borrow heavily from the opening riff on 'Bangin' for their massive worldwide hit, 'Bad Medicine'.

Far Far Away

This is Noddy and Don's favourite Slade song of all their many recordings. A massive drum from Don introduces a slow shuffle of acoustic guitars and irresistible sing-a-long choruses. Jim's bass playing is worthy of special note as he dive-bombs up and down the neck of his guitar to delivery the catchy underlying riffs. This reached No. 2 on the UK chart in October 1974. The Ford Motor Company would later use Far Far Away in an advertising campaign for Transit vans.

How Does It Feel?

One of the greatest moments of Slade's entire career, this ballad shows Slade in an altogether different mood. It's a tour-de -orce of dynamic musical moods. Written for the movie *Flame*, the band needed something that would work in a cinematic environment; it had to be dynamic and effective in a variety of ways. They tailor-made the song for the film; the quieter moments counterbalanced by some gigantic riffs. A brass section was added, too.

Noddy has never sounded better. The song was an absolute triumph but unfortunately it only reached No. 15 on the chart. Here, they prove their facility for gentle melody and delicate delivery. Noel Gallagher was quoted as saying, 'People just think when they listen to Slade, they think of "C'mon Feel The Noize" and "Mama Weer All Crazy Now," but "How Does It Feel?" is easily one of the best songs ever written, ever! That is such a brilliant song… Go and buy it!'

Thanks For The Memory

In May 1975 this slightly frivolous single reached No. 7 on the British chart. It bounces along quite happily as Noddy shouts, 'Thanks for the memory, thanks for it all/Wham, bam, thank you mam, thanks for the ball!' It signalled a fall from grace that at one point had been unthinkable. The automatic hits had begun to falter.

Let's Call It Quits

Featuring a rip-roaring vocal from Noddy that is truly awe-inspiring, the groove is reminiscent of Dave Edmunds' early Seventies hit, 'I Hear You Knocking'. 'Quits' only reached No. 11 on the UK chart, which was a major blow to the band. It spelled the end of their run of hits in the Seventies.

My, Oh My

This was the song that brought Slade triumphantly back to the charts in the Eighties. Here, we have an anthem-like workout with the band at their sing-a-long best. 'My, Oh My' stormed up the chart and reached No. 2 in November 1983.

Run, Run Away

The band had their first Top 20 US hit with this single, which reached No. 7 on the UK singles chart. With this track Slade had finally received the success that was so overdue. Another sing-a-long special, this time with a 'Big Country' flavour, harmony guitars abound and there's a tricky groove change too that adds a nice lilting feel to the whole proceedings.

The video for 'Run, Run Away' was was a staple on MTV. Nevertheless, it was Slade's last real hit.

AFTERWORD

Alan's story

When it comes to music, I'm the original early starter at the tender age of eight. While a large number of my peers were busy discussing what Colonel Steve Austin's next adventure might be in *The Six Million Dollar Man*, or whether such a thing existed as a planet that Dr Who hadn't visited, in another part of the schoolyard I had my face buried in a magazine, dreaming about one day becoming a rock star. I'd live in a huge house, have a solid gold Rolls Royce, marry one of Pan's People or the girl who presented *Magpie*, and have my face on the cover of *Look-In* magazine. All right, so at eight these things do need a wee bit of fine tuning!

It had all started a year earlier with a single slab of vinyl. the record in question being 'Blockbuster' by Sweet, a song that started with a loud siren. At the time the only room with a hi-fi at my parents' house was facing the street, right on the front. So many times I returned to the living room, only for my Mum to ask, 'Where was that ambulance going in such a hurry?' The simple answer was nowhere: it was all contained in the grooves.

For about a year leading up to the end of 1972 my brother and me (he was all of one year my junior) compiled a decent collection of singles via Saturday afternoon trips into town with Dad. This collection included records by The Sweet, Mud, The Glitter Band, David Essex, The Arrows and Marc Bolan, to name but a few. At the back of this

Left: Slade at Earl's Court in 1973.

motley selection lurked a single in a bright red generic Polydor Records bag, entitled 'Gudbuy T' Jane.' It was the tenth commercial single release by a bunch of geezers from the Black Country, who collectively answered to the name Slade – though at the time our only knowledge of them was that (a) the lead singer wore a big hat, (b) the lead guitarist looked silly and (c) they couldn't spell. The latter only served to bring them closer to me. Having been one of the last batch to learn to spell on the old ITA system, I didn't actually know they were spelling anything wrong at all. Diagnosed as dyslexic at the age of eleven, I thought Graham was spelt Gram for three years – and it's my middle name!

With the arrival of the album *Slayed!* and as if overnight Slade became a firm favourite. Between the ages of eleven and fourteen I had written the word 'Slade' on my hand in black marker far too often for it to be considered healthy. Within a year the bedroom I shared with my brother was plastered in Slade posters. Though the actual walls were painted cream any number of visits wouldn't have helped you in finding that one out.

Before I go any further I should point out that when we were kids Dad was not what you'd call a big one for planning ahead. If it's happening tomorrow, we can sort it out today; in this way a large number of family holiday destinations were sprung on us, Mum included, on a Friday night as we travelled Saturday morning.

At this stage in my life I had no idea that you could actually go and see groups play live – *Look-*

Afterword

In wasn't best known for its gig guide. I thought you watched groups on TV. *Top Of The Pops* and *Supersonic* were the highlight of my week. One evening in the summer of 1973 in walked Dad with a big grin on his face. 'I've bought four tickets for the Slade show in town tonight,' he announced. Mum looked up from the paper and calmly announced that she wasn't going. My brother and I thought it was incredible; phone calls were made and at the twenty-third hour my Uncle Keith stepped up to the challenge. That night Slade played a blinding set – though they were incredibly loud. I'll give you a clue just how loud they were: sat in the front row of the balcony David and I had our hands over both ears all night and never missed a note, while my poor uncle was in the doctor's surgery first thing the next morning to complain about the ringing in his ears. Asked whether he'd seen Slade the previous night, he told them yes, and was given the same advice as everybody through the door that same morning: just go home, it will get better! 'Skweeze Me Pleeze Me' was released around the same time, and effortlessly sailed to the top of the charts.

Very soon, again via *Look-In,* word got out that Slade were about to star in their own movie. My first encounter with *Flame* was a paperback book I bought from Seed & Gabutts book store in Blackburn, Lancashire. The novel of the movie turned out to be a story far removed from the one that reached the big screen. It was, if memory serves, a lot grittier and contained quite an amount of bad language. But as no one other than me had

Mud, walking in like dynamite!

actually read the book, it didn't take much asking to persuade Dad to take us to see the movie, and to say we loved it was an understatement. That year *Slade In Flame*, the soundtrack album, probably got played more than other album in the Parker household. By the time Christmas arrived it was in need of renewal.

With the advent of punk rock a lot of the glam bands simply disappeared. Some of them called it a day, while others drifted into a career of cabaret or the Pontins/Butlins circuit. Slade had been in the USA and returned just in time for the outbreak of punk, but they didn't allow this new musical movement to affect them. For my money *Nobody's Fools* is a great album filled with killer tunes, and if I'm honest I love the cover too: it fits perfectly, job done. I saw Slade play live again before their huge Reading comeback, this time in a Blackburn nightclub. Once again they raised the roof.

Anyone who's read any of my previous work will no doubt be aware that punk stole my soul, hook, line and sinker. But as I once told *Terrorizer* magazine that if you show me a Northern punk rocker who didn't own at least two Slade albums first, I'll show you a liar – and I'll stick to that to the grave.

But no matter how many incredible punk albums I listened to, or gigs I attended, I always had time for

Dave fixes Pot Noodles in Alan's Kitchen.

The Ballroom Blitz Kids, Sweet.

Slade. What happened next pretty much sets the two musicical forms in stone for me. During a Stiff Little Fingers after-show party at the Brixton Academy in the late Eighties I met Mark Brennan, currently the owner of Captain Oi! Records. At the time Mark was a partner in Link Music. We talked about books and sleeve-notes for albums. Mark organised a meeting at Receiver Records and later that week I met Frank Lea. Over the best part of the next 17 years I worked on various projects with Frank, and we always found time to talk about Slade. I mean, by now I'm having regular coffee meetings with Jim's brother: the 12-year-old Slade fan inside me would have run a country mile first! I only discovered Whild through Frank, and I've played that CD to death.

After years of magazine work, touring with bands and writing sleeve-notes, in 1999 I decided a change was way overdue. A friend handed me a copy of *The Stage* magazine, which contained an advert placed by Judy Totton Publicity. The company was looking for a new press officer and my friend said I should apply. Why not give it a go? Within a matter of weeks I'd got the job and after a few months working there Judy arrived one morning with the news that Dave Hill had been in contact, and was looking for a press officer. My world span.

A few days later Dave turned up at the office. He was incredibly fun to work with, a genuine guy who was up for pretty much everything offered to him. It wasn't long before I'd also met Don Powell and caught Slade 2 live.

One crazy day I had a call from *Front* magazine rang, wondering if Dave would do a Top 10 instant soup chart – given that Vic Reeves and Bob Mortimer had been doing a sketch about Slade for what seemed like years, the punch line of which always seemed to have something to do with various flavours of Cup-a-Soup. Dave thought the idea was hilarious so we organised the shoot in my kitchen – yeah, a member of Slade in *my kitchen*! The lads from *Front* and me played *Old, New, Borrowed And Blue* so many times that night I think even the neighbours knew the words. And to this day there is still a photograph of Dave holding a Pot Noodle in my kitchen and (apologies to anyone who's already seen this coming) whenever anyone comes round they say, 'That's Dave Hill in this kitchen!'

This book has truly been a labour of love. Without owning 'Gudbuy T' Jane', without attending my first Slade gig in 1973, without seeing *Flame* on the big screen or owning that collection of incredible albums I don't know what I'd be doing now – but I do know it wouldn't be anything like this.

Steve's story

Slade were entertainment, pure and simple. Every time I saw them I was amazed at how good they really were. They didn't have 'rock as art' pretensions, they blasted out nuclear-powered-vandal-rock and I loved it!

To me Slade epitomise the early Seventies, my favourite decade. I have so many great memories of that time – the enormous feeling of optimism that engulfed me then, and Slade were there at every turn! 'LOOK WOT YOU DUN'.

I was lucky enough to get a Chopper bike as a present one Christmas and I treasured it. I loved riding around on that thing in my Parka. 'MERRY CHRISTMAS EVERYBODY'.

Wednesday night was *The Sweeney* night on TV. The next day I'd go to school and we would all discuss the programme. We loved the fighting and swearing. On Saturday nights there was the US cop show *Starsky and Hutch*, comedy with *Morecambe and Wise*, and chat with *Parkinson*. 'FAR, FAR AWAY'.

In the week on television we had *Magpie*, *The Tomorrow People*, *Bless This House* with Sid James, *Man About The House*, *The Six Million Dollar Man*, *Budgie* starring Adam Faith and *Vision On*.

The Gods of Glam Rock!

Sunday afternoons were *Catweazle* and Roger Moore and Tony Curtis in *The Persuaders*. These were interspersed with adverts: 'For Mash Get Smash!' 'You Hum It Son, I'll Play It!' 'Don't Talk! Eat!' 'Splash It All Over!' 'TAKE ME BAK 'OME'.

The TV adverts were as entertaining as the programmes themselves, and I loved the music that accompanied the Old Spice aftershave advert. Hi Karate was also popular and I fancied the buxom woman who featured in them. The Cadbury's 'Flake' adverts were always interesting to a teenage lad, too! 'GUDBUY T' JANE'.

I wanted to go and see *The Exorcist*, the X-certificate horror movie I had read so much about in the Sunday papers. It was billed as the scariest film ever released, and a huge furore surrounded the movie. I was too young, so I didn't get to see it. 'COZ I LUV YOU'.

I also wanted to see *A Clockwork Orange* which was also immersed in controversy but I was too young to see that, too. 'MY FRIEND STAN'.

And then there was *Enter The Dragon*. This featured my hero of the time, Bruce Lee, but due to the extensive violence it was X-certificate, too, so I couldn't get in to see that either. 'BANGIN' MAN'.

However, I went to see *Flame* three times. No problem there! It was fantastic. I loved it. 'HOW DOES IT FEEL?'

Thursday nights at 7.30 on BBC1, straight after *Tomorrow's World* my world would come alive with *Top Of The Pops*. I'd have to sit through Gilbert O'Sullivan, Chickory Tip and the Wombles just to get to Slade, who thankfully were constantly on the show. I would sit and imagine just what it must be like to be in the band. 'EVERYDAY'. And then there

was Pan's People, the resident *Top Of The Pops* dancers. 'THANKS FOR THE MEMORY'.

The awful Austin Allegro, or 'all aggro' cars were popular and seemed to be everywhere, but occasionally you would catch a glimpse of the magical Jensen Interceptor with its state-of-the-art eight-track cartridge player. 'CUM ON FEEL THE NOIZE'.

I committed many a fashion crime, as did the whole population. Platform shoes, massive collars and three-button high waistband flares were the order of the day. 'MAMA WEER ALL CRAZEE NOW'.

I would play my records on my GEC 'music centre' and listen to the charts every Sunday evening. 'SKWEEZE ME PLEEZE ME'.

It may be a cliché, but with the passing of time their stature has justifiably grown – but not nearly enough. It must be remembered that Slade created a blueprint for a whole new genre of rock music, one which has influenced every subsequent generation. Take a bow Mötley Crüe, Poison, Guns 'n' Roses, Quiet Riot, Bon Jovi, Oasis, Aerosmith, Kiss... the list goes on and on.

Slade have given us some of the most enduring rock'n'roll songs of all time, and their contribution to rock music is enormous and unquestionable. They were massively underestimated and criminally overlooked. I just hope this book will help to redress the balance and put Slade in their rightful place in pop history: at the top, where they belong.

Slade kept the whole thing simple. They chanted. They screamed. They rocked. They partied. They had great songs. They had fun. They entertained. They were a great band and they belong to YOU AND ME! 'GET DOWN AND GET WITH IT'.

SLADE TRIVIA QUIZ

1   Which major rock band asked Noddy Holder to join them after their own lead singer tragically died?

2   Which Slade song did punk rock band The Stranglers often play on stage?

3   Who said, 'Noddy Holder's got one of the greatest voices in rock ever!'?

4   Which comedian, writer and West End musical impresario is a huge Slade fan?

5   Who is Dave Hill's favourite singer?

6   Which song did Noddy Holder always wish he had written?

7   What is Jim Lea's favourite book?

8   Which Radio DJ and massive Slade fan finished writing his 'Slade Musical' in January 2005?

9   What is Don Powell's favourite comedy TV show?

10   Dave Hill is left-handed but plays his guitar right-handed. True or false?

11   Which member of the band once drove a car into a swimming pool?

12   Which member of Slade appeared in the BBC TV adaptation of *Lorna Doone* at Christmas 2000?

13   Who used to confidently boast to Slade, with no trace of shame, 'I'm going to be a famous pop star one day. I'm going to be bigger than you guys'?

14   Who was Noddy Holder's favourite male singer in the 1970's?

15   Which punk rock band regularly attend Slade's London shows?

16   Jim Lea was born in the back of a car. True or false?

17   What is Noddy Holder's favourite book?

18   Who said, 'If you notice, around 1972 I started doing much different music. I couldn't do the heavy rock thing any more. Noddy Holder was around kicking every singer in the ass. I never wanted to be a pop singer. Christ, how I hated Noddy!'

19   Who was Dave Hill's favourite band in the 1970's?

20   Who is Noddy Holder's favourite female singer?

Left: Nod back on Top of the Pops.

1 AC/DC **2** 'Gudbuy T'Jane', **3** Ozzy Osbourne **4** Sir Ben Elton **5** John Lennon **6** Robert Palmer's 'Addicted To Love', **7** George Orwell's *Animal Farm* **8** Mike Read **9** *Fawlty Towers* **10** True **11** Noddy Holder **12** Don Powell **13** Freddy Mercury; he was not in a band at the time but would indeed go on to be a famous pop star with the super-group Queen **14** Joe Cocker **15** The Damned **16** False. He was actually born in a public house **17** *Catch 22* **18** Tom Jones **19** Reggae band Osibisa **20** Aretha Franklin

DISCOGRAPHY

Singles

Genesis/Roach Daddy

1969

Wild Winds Are Blowing/
One Way Hotel

Shape Of Things To Come/
C'mon C'mon

1970

Know Who You Are/
Dapple Rose

Get Down And Get With
It/Do You Want Me/Gospel
According To Rasputin

1971

Coz I Luv You/My Life Is
Natural

Look Wot You Dun/
Candidate

1972

Take Me Bak 'Ome/
Wonderin' Y

Mama Weer All Crazee
Now/Man Who Speeks Evil

Gudbuy T' Jane/I Won't Let
It 'Appen Agen

Cum On Feel The Noize/
I'm Mee I'm Now And
That's Orl

1973

Skweeze Me Pleeze Me/
Kill 'Em At The Hot Club
Tonite

My Friend Stan/My Town

Merry Christmas
Everybody/Don't Blame Me

Everyday/Good Time Gals

1974

The Bangin' Man/She Did
It To Me

Far, Far Away/OK Yesterday
Was Yesterday

How Does It Feel?/So Far
So Good

1975

Thanks For The Memory/
Raining In My Champagne

In For A Penny/Can You
Just Imagine

Let's Call It Quits/When
The Chips Are Down

1976

Nobody's Fool/LA Jinx
Gypsy Roadhog/Forest Full
Of Needles

1977

Burning In The Heat Of
Love/Ready Steady Kids

My Baby Left Me/Ohms
Give Us A Goal/Daddio

1978

Rock'n' Roll Bolero/It's
Alright By Me

Ginny Ginny/Dizzy Mama

Sign Of The Times/Not
Tonight Josephine

1979

Okey Cokey/My Baby's
Got It

Slade Alive! At Reading (EP)

1980

We'll bring The House
Down/Hold On To Your
Hats

1981

Wheels Ain't Coming
Down/Not Tonight
Josephine

Knuckle Sandwich Nancy/
I'mad

Lock Up Your Daughters/
Sign Of The Times

Ruby Red/Punk, Funk &
Junk/Rock'n'Roll Preacher
(live)/Take Me Bak 'Ome
(live)

1982

(And Now The Waltz) C'est
La Vie/Merry Christmas
Everybody (live)

Okey Cokey/Get Down And
Get With It

My, Oh My/Keep Your
Hands Off My Power
Supply/Don't Tame A
Hurricane

1983

Run, Run Away/Two-Track
Stereo, One-Track Mind

1984

All Join Hands/Here's To
Seven Year Bitch/Leave
Them Girls Alone

1985

Myzsterious Miszter Jones/
Mama Nature Is A Rocker

Do You Believe In
Miracles?/My Oh My

Still the Same/Gotta Go
Home

1987

That's What Friends Are
For/Wild Wild Party

We Won't Give In/Ooh La
La In LA

Let's Dance/Standing On
The Corner

1988

Radio Wall Of Sound/Lay
Your Love On The Line

1991

Universe/Red Hot/Merry
Christmas Everybody

Albums

**BEGINNINGS aka BALLZY
in the USA (1969)**

Genesis

Everybody's Next One

Knocking Nails Into
My House

Roach Daddy

Ain't Got No Heart

Pity The Mother

Mad Dog Cole

Fly Me High

If This World Were Mine

Martha My Dear

Born To Be Wild

Journey To The Centre
Of My Mind

PLAY IT LOUD (1970)

Raven

See Us Here

Dapple Rose

Could I

One-Way Hotel

The Shape Of Things
To Come

Know Who You Are

I Remember

Pouk Hill

Angelina

Dirty Joker

Sweet Box

SLADE ALIVE! (1972)

Hear Me Calling

In Like A Shot From My Gun

Darling Be Home Soon

Know Who You Are

Keep On Rocking

Get Down And Get With It

Born To Be Wild

SLAYED? (1972)

How D'You Ride?

The Whole World's Goin'
Crazee

Look At Last Nite

I Won't Let It 'Appen Again

Move Over

Gudbuy T' Jane

Gudbuy Gudbuy

Mama Weer All Crazee Now

I Don' Mind

Let The Good Times Roll

SLADEST (1973)

Cum On Feel The Noize

Look Wot You Dun

Gudbuy T'Jane

One-Way Hotel

Skweeze Me, Pleeze Me

Pouk Hill

The Shape Of Things To
Come

Take Me Bak 'Ome

Coz I Luv You

Wild Winds Are Blowin'

Know Who You Are

Get Down And Get With It

Look At Last Nite

Mama Weer All Crazee Now

**OLD, NEW, BORROWED
AND BLUE (1974)
aka STOMP YOUR HANDS
AND CLAP YOUR FEET
in the USA**

Just A Little Bit

When The Lights Are Out

My Town

Find Yourself A Rainbow

Miles Out To Sea

We're Really Gonna Raise
The Roof

Do We Still Do It?

How Can It Be?

Don't Blame Me

My Friend Stan

Everyday

Good Time Gals

SLADE IN FLAME (1974)

How Does It Feel?

Them Kinda Monkeys Can't
Swing

So Far So Good

Summer Song (Wishing You
Were Here)

OK Yesterday Was Yesterday

Far Far Away

This Girl

Lay It Down

Heaven Knows

Standin' On The Corner

NOBODY'S FOOLS (1976)

Nobody's Fools

Do The Dirty

Let's Call It Quits

Pack Up Your Troubles

In For A Penny

Get On Up

LA Jinx

Did Ya Mama Ever Tell Ya

Scratch My Back

I'm A Talker

All The World Is A Stage

**WHATEVER HAPPENED TO
SLADE? (1977)**

Be

Lightning Never Strikes Back

Gypsy Roadhog

Dogs Of Vengeance

When Fantasy Calls

One-Eyed Jacks With
Moustaches

Big Apple Blues

Dead Men Tell No Tales

She's Got The Lot

It Ain't Love But It Ain't Bad

The Soul, The Roll And The
Motion

**SLADE ALIVE VOLUME 2
(1978)**

Get On Up

Take Me Bak 'Ome

My Baby Left Me

Be

Mama Weer All Crazee Now

Burning In The Heat Of Love

Everyday

Gudbuy T' Jane

One-Eyed Jacks With
Moustaches

C'mon Feel The Noize

RETURN TO BASE (1979)

Wheels Ain't Comin' Down

Hold On To Your Hats

Chakeeta

Don't Waste Your Time

Sign Of The Times

I'm A Rocker

Nuts, Bolts And Screws

My Baby's Got It

I'm Mad

Lemme Love Into Ya

Ginny Ginny

**WE'LL BRING THE HOUSE
DOWN (1980)**

We'll Bring The House Down

Night Starvation

Wheels Ain't Coming Down

Hold On To Your Hats

When I'm Dancin' I Ain't
Fightin'

Dizzy Mama

Nuts, Bolts And Screws

My Baby's Got It

Lemme Love Into Ya

I'm A Rocker

**TILL DEAF DO US PART
(1981)**

Rock And Roll Preacher
(Hallelujah I'm On Fire)

Lock Up Your Daughters

Till Deaf Do Us Part

Ruby Red

She Brings Out The Devil
In Me

A Night To Remember

M'Hat, M'Coat

It's Your Body Not Your
Mind

Let The Rock Roll Out Of
Control

That Was No Lady That Was
My Wife

Knuckle Sandwich Nancy

Till Deaf Resurrected

ON STAGE (1982)

Rock And Roll Preacher

When I'm Dancin' I Ain't
Fightin'

Take Me Bak 'Ome

Everyday

Lock Up Your Daughters

We'll Bring The House Down

A Night To Remember

Gudbuy T' Jane

Mama Weer All Crazee Now

You'll Never Walk Alone

**THE AMAZING KAMIKAZE
SYNDROME (1983)**

Slam The Hammer Down

In The Doghouse

Run Runaway

High And Dry

My, Oh My

Cocky Rock Boys (Rule OK)

Ready To Explode

I: The Warm Up

II: The Grid

III: The Race

IV: The Dream

(And Now – The Waltz) C'est
La Vie

Cheap 'N' Nasty Luv

Razzle Dazzle Man

**KEEP YOUR HANDS OFF
MY POWER SUPPLY
(1984)**

Run Run Away

My, Oh My

High And Dry

Slam The Hammer Down

In The Doghouse

Keep Your Hands Off My
Power Supply

Cheap 'N' Nasty Luv

Can't Tame A Hurricane

(And Now The Waltz) C'est
La Vie

Ready To Explode

ROGUES GALLERY (1985)

Hey Ho Wish You Well

Little Sheila

Harmony

Myzsterious Mizster Jones

Walking On Water, Running
On Alcohol

Seven Year Bitch

I'll Be There

I Win, You Lose

Time To Rock

All Join Hands

**YOU BOYZ MAKE BIG
NOIZE (1987)**

Love Is Like A Rock

That's What Friends Are For

Still The Same

Fools Go Crazy

She's Heavy

We Won't Give In

Won't You Rock With Me

Ooh La La In LA

Me And The Boys

Sing Shout (Knock Yourself
Out)

The Roaring Silence

It's Hard Having Fun
Nowadays

WALL OF HITS (1991)

Get Down And Get With It

Coz I Luv You

Look Wot You Dun

Take Me Bak 'Ome

Mama Weer All Crazee Now

Gudbuy T'Jane

Cum On Feel The Noize

Skweeze Me, Pleeze Me

My Friend Stan

Everyday

Bangin' Man
Far, Far Away
How Does It Feel?
Thanks For The Memory
    (Wham Bam Thank You
    Mam)
Let's Call It Quits
My, Oh My
Run, Run Away
Radio Wall Of Sound
Universe
Merry Christmas Everybody

**THE VERY BEST OF SLADE
(2005)**
Disc 1:
Get Down And Get With It
Coz I Love You
Look What You Dun
Take Me Bak 'Ome
Mama Weer All Crazee Now
Gudbuy T'Jane
Cum On Feel The Noize
Skweeze Me Pleeze Me
My Friend Stan
Everyday
The Bangin' Man
Far, Far Away
How Does It Feel?
Thanks For The Memory
    (Wham Bham Thank You
    Mam)
In For A Penny
Let's Call It Quits
Well Bring The House Down
My, Oh My
Run Run Away
Merry Christmas Everybody

Disc 2:
All Join Hands
Gypsy Roadhog
My Baby Left Me – That's All
    Right
Lock Up Your Daughters
Wheels Ain't Coming Down
Born To Be Wild
Ruby Red
(And Now – The Waltz) C'est
    La Vie
Seven Year Bitch
Myzsterious Mizster Jones
Do You Believe In Miracles?
Still The Same

Radio Wall Of Sound
Universe

*Slade had 16 Top 20 hits
between 1971 and 1976,
including six No. 1's, three
of which went straight in
at the top. They achieved
three No. 2's and two No.
3's. Slade sold more singles
in the UK than any other
Seventies group, and no
other British pop act of
the Seventies enjoyed such
massive success in the UK
charts. The Beatles had
22 Top Ten records in the
Sixties, and Slade came
closest to emulating this in
the Seventies.*

**Recordings That
Include Slade Members
The Vendors, The 'N
Betweens and The
Mavericks**

The Vendors
Don't Leave Me Now
Twilight Time
Take Your Time
Peace Pipe
    Only 'Don't Leave Me Now'
was penned by Hill/Howells.
The Vendors recorded four
songs still known to exist to
this day in 1964 (these made
up a privately pressed EP on
Domino Records).
John Howells: Vocals
Mick Marson: Rhythm Guitar
Dave Hill: Lead Guitar
Don Powell: Drums
Unknown: Bass Guitar

**Steve Brett and the
Mavericks**
Wishing
Anything That's Part of You
(Columbia Records DB7470)
Sad, Lonely & Blue
Candy
(Columbia Records DB7581)
Chains On My Heart

Sugar Shack
(Columbia Records DB7794)
Hurting Inside
    The first six of these
represent the A- and B-sides
of three singles issued by
Columbia Records in 1965;
the latter was an un-issued
demo. Steve Brett wrote all
the original A-sides.
Steve Brett: Vocals, Guitar
Phil Burnell: Rhythm Guitar
Pete Bickley: Bass Guitar
**Noddy Holder: Guitar,
Vocals**
Gerry Kibble: Drums
Terry Taylor: Saxophone

The 'N Betweens (Mk. 1)
Can Your Monkey Do the
Dog?
Respectable
I Wish You Would
Ooh Poo Pa Doo
    These tracks featured on a
private acetate from 1965.
Feel So Fine
Take A Heart
Little Nightingale
You Don't Believe Me
    These tracks were featured
on a Barclay Records EP
number 70907 in 1965.
John Howells: Vocals
Mick Marson: Rhythm Guitar
Dave 'Cass' Jones: Bass Guitar
Don Powell: Drums
Dave Hill: Lead Guitar

The 'N Betweens (Mk. 2)
Security
Evil Witchman
    This was a promotional
release through Highland
Records in the US in 1966.
You Better Run
Evil Witchman
    This was a Columbia
Records single DB8080 from
December 1966.
Hold Tight
Ugly Girl *
Need *
These last two feature on an

unreleased 1966 demo.
**Noddy Holder: Vocals,
Guitar**
Dave Hill: Lead Guitar
Jim Lea: Bass Guitar
Don Powell: Drums
Kim Fowley: Additional
Vocals

DVD Guide
Flame (Union Square
Pictures USPDVD001)
Full-length wide screen print
of the movie, Noddy Holder
interview by Gary Crowley,
London 2002, photo gallery
and full discography.

Inside Slade (Classic Rock
Productions CRL1586)
59 minute 'independent
critical review', too much
talk, not enough music.
This product was released
unauthorised.

The Very Best Of Slade
(Polydor/Universal 9834801)
Featuring: Wall Of Hits (14
official promo clips), Set Of
Six – Live (Granada TV),
More Hits (Six TV clips) and
a commentary from Noddy,
Jim, Dave & Don.

**Max & Paddy's Road
to Nowhere** (Channel 4
C4DVD10010)
The entire first series of the
comedy TV show featuring
Peter Kay and Patrick
McGuinness.
    Noddy Holder makes a
guest appearance as Mick
Bustin' in Episode 2; his
character is a mechanic and
he owns a garage. The door
features a cartoon logo not
unlike the one featured in the
Ghostbusters movie, featuring
the legend, 'Who you gonna
call… Mick Bustin.' His two
burly assistants are named
'Les' and 'Dennis'.